A FAMILY Affair

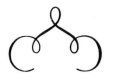

A
FAMILY
Affair

India Under Three
Prime Ministers

VED MEHTA

New York   Oxford
OXFORD UNIVERSITY PRESS
1982

Library of Congress Cataloging in Publication Data
Mehta, Ved, 1934–
A family affair.
1. India—Politics and government—1947– I. Title.
DS480.84.M379 954.04 81–22508
ISBN 0–19–503118–0 AACR2

The contents of this book originally appeared in
The New Yorker in somewhat different form.

Printing (last digit): 9 8 7 6 5 4 3 2 1

Printed in the United States of America

TO HILARY AND HELGE RUBINSTEIN

A Family Affair is a sequel to *The New India,* published in 1978. Taken together, the two books recount the political history of India from Independence, in 1947, to the present, and, as such, they highlight the doings and supposed doings of a few leaders, their parents, their children, their grandchildren, their in-laws, and sundry other collaterals. This is not really surprising: in a sense, a study of Indian politics has to be a study of the shifting power and influence of its ruling families and their close and distant relatives, for although India is the world's largest parliamentary democracy, modelled on that of Westminster, it is also a traditional feudal society, organized around the principles of caste and family.

This book has been in the making since 1977. In the various stages of writing, rewriting, and revising, I received help, at one time or another, from Naomi Grob, Harriet Walden and her typing pool, Nandini Mehta, Eleanor Gould Packard, Amolak Ram Mehta, and William Shawn. Here I can only express my deep appreciation and gratitude to them all.

New York   V.M.
October, 1981

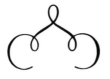

Contents

PROLOGUE

The Elephant

In June, 1977, during one of my annual visits to India, the front pages of the newspapers in New Delhi were taken up for some days with the fate of an elephant named Sunderkali—carrying huge pictures and running banner headlines such as "CAN ANY-ONE SAVE SUNDERKALI?," " 'TRUNK CALL' FOR MERCY," "SUNDERKALI DIES AFTER GETTING ON HER FEET." The news stories concerned a thirty-two-year-old cow elephant that over the years had paraded in a Republic Day pageant and, festooned with posters and contraceptive devices, had ambled about the city advertising medical remedies and spreading the gospel of family planning. One day, she had tripped and broken a leg, and after hobbling around for four weeks had buckled and lain down on a roadside near a bridge. Her mahout was distraught—his very livelihood depended on her—but, try as he might, he could not get her to raise herself. A crowd of passersby began keeping vigil by her side, and fortune-tellers, homeopaths, and practitioners of ancient Ayur-Vedic medicine flocked to her and tried their arts. The central government began issuing regular medical bulletins on the elephant's condition. The then Minister of Agriculture, Surjit Singh Barnala, ordered his officials to see that she was given the best treatment in the government's power.

Specialists and surgeons were summoned from hundreds of miles around—from veterinary hospitals, agricultural colleges, great zoos. They operated on her leg and set it in a cast; a crane and a steel assembly raised her to her feet. She stood unassisted for two hours, and then had a heart attack and died. "Sunderkali was as much a friend of the high and mighty as she was of the slum dwellers," commented a leading national English-language daily, the *Statesman*.

At the same time, New Delhi, like much of the country, was preoccupied with a severe power shortage. The electrical system routinely sloughed off sections of the city by turns, plunging them for between two and four hours a day into hot, still, rancid darkness, like the inside of a dead elephant's mouth. The fans would slow down and stop, and flies would land in swarms and stick to the skin; refrigerators would go off, and foods would spoil; water pumps would quit, and the toilets wouldn't work. The privileged owners of these modern conveniences would pounce on their newspapers as eagerly for the load-shedding schedules as for the weather report, and scan the skies for a sign of rain; they had always looked forward to the monsoon rain, which would cool the air, even if it did spawn countless varieties of crawling and flying insects, but now they were learning that the rain also fed hydroelectric power plants. And even when there was electricity the use of air-conditioners was banned during the day. Inspectors roamed the streets and checked for violators, who could have their electricity shut down for four days and nights. By nine o'clock in the evening, however, when the appetite of industry was appeased, air-conditioners everywhere might be turned on; people who had perhaps spent the day making visits to relatives or friends on a different load-shedding schedule, looking for a fan and an iced drink, could finally be at rest at home.

The load shedding was indiscriminate, sparing neither houses nor shops, neither offices nor factories, neither railway stations

ns. It was nothing less than power famine, conjuring
st of pre-British village India and warning that the
powered city, with its air-cooled shops and offices,
ly lines, its traffic lights, its trains, was much more
fragile than the ancient, mudlamp-lit village of the poor. For a
few hours, the temporary victims of load shedding and the permanent victims of poverty were united by their sweat, and they
might as well have belonged to the same class. The looting and
arson that accompanied, say, the blackout in New York in July,
1977, were unknown, because the Indian poor still have an
of a ss of community and God, and live under the injunction
of a atalistic moral code. In fact, a fuss over a New York-style
bla out would make no sense in the Indian context, because
co red with the poor of, say, Old Delhi's Jama Masjid the
m poor live in unimaginable affluence, and arousing sympa-
them would be like trying to arouse sympathy for someone
headache in someone dying of a brain tumor. The onset
monsoon rain obviated load shedding, and people quickly
that, with the passing of the years, Indian power shortages
ecome increasingly widespread, acute, and frequent.

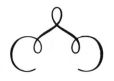

A
FAMILY
Affair

1

Mother
and Son

Indian politics since Independence has been bedevilled by the relationships of father and daughter, mother and son, father and son, father-in-law and son-in-law, and husband and wife. It was thought that Jawaharlal Nehru, who served as the first Prime Minister of the newly independent India for seventeen years, until his death, in 1964, had ambivalent feelings about whether his only child, Indira Gandhi, should succeed him as Prime Minister. On the one hand, he seemed to have groomed her for the office: he permitted her to live with him in the Prime Minister's residence, to become his official hostess (he was a widower), to become his unofficial secretary and his confidante; although she was elected to no office and held no position in the government, he helped her assume an ever more important behind-the-scenes role in party politics, and finally, in 1959 and 1960, she served, in part thanks to him, as the president of the ruling Congress Party. On the other hand, Nehru seemed to have been alert to the danger of setting a precedent of family succession and so perhaps giving rise to a Nehru dynasty: he frequently warned his colleagues to be on guard against his own dictatorial tendencies; he labored to foster India's nascent democratic traditions; and he saw to it that, in the end, his successor was chosen by free and open methods.

Nehru was succeeded by Lal Bahadur Shastri, who was as plebeian and orthodox in outlook as Nehru had been patrician and Western. Shastri, however, was Prime Minister for less than two years; he died suddenly in 1966. There were several strong contenders for his office, but the Congress Party bosses were unable to agree on any one of them. Almost by default, they selected Mrs. Gandhi—and for the very same reason, it appeared, that Nehru had ruled her out: she was the patriarch's daughter. They expected that she would be mostly a figurehead, and that they would be able to govern in her name, but instead she made their behind-the-scenes power an issue, taking them by surprise. As a result, she was able to overthrow them in 1969, and capture control of the Congress Party. The Old Guard, unable to do anything else about it, pointedly began calling itself the Old Congress Party.

No sooner had Mrs. Gandhi become a leader in her own right, in 1969, than the father-and-daughter theme gave way to a mother-and-son theme. Mrs. Gandhi, at the time she assumed office, was a forty-nine-year-old widow (her husband had died in 1960) with two children, both sons. While her older son, Rajiv, had never openly shown much interest in politics, the doings of her younger son, Sanjay, perpetually haunted her career.

Sanjay was son of the best-known political family in the country. His home was almost always the Prime Minister's residence. (His grandfather and his mother, between them, have served as Prime Minister of India for all but four of the years that India has been independent, and Sanjay and Rajiv continued to live with their mother even after they married and had children.) He went to some of the most expensive private schools the country had to offer. He finished school but never attended a university. From childhood, he had a passion for cars, and he received training as a car mechanic at what was probably the world's best car company—the Rolls-Royce factory in Britain. In 1970, when he was almost twenty-four, he was given one of the nation's most coveted industrial licenses by the Ministry of Industries of Mrs. Gandhi's government—a license to manufacture and sell cars. He claimed that his car would be a "people's car," small, inexpensive, and entirely of Indian manufacture—a sort of Indian version of the Volkswagen. He said that it would be within the means of ordinary people. (The cars then being produced in India contained many imported parts and were extremely expensive—beyond the reach even of many well-to-do Indians.) He named his intended car the Maruti, after the son of a Hindu wind god, and floated a public company called Maruti, Ltd. At the time, it was charged in the press and in Parliament that the granting of this license to the son of the Prime Minister, a young man with no business experience and with no known capital of his own, was blatant nepotism—especially since the socialist governments of Nehru and Mrs. Gandhi had previously denied such licenses to well-established companies.

Many critics of "the son" were people who had vociferously supported Mrs. Gandhi's becoming Prime Minister on the ground that she was Nehru's daughter and was therefore the person best equipped to carry on her father's tradition. The outcry against Sanjay's license continued for years, but Mrs. Gandhi was so firmly in control of the Congress Party that for much of that time she was able mostly to ignore it. But eventually Sanjay's Maruti—or, rather, the absence of it—became one of Mrs. Gandhi's major political problems.

As it happened, the early phase of the controversy over Sanjay's obtaining the license for the Maruti coincided with three years of drought, with an unbroken period of rising prices, and with widespread student and worker agitation. During this period, a small-time local politician named Raj Narain, who had stood as a nuisance candidate for Parliament in Mrs. Gandhi's home constituency of Rae Bareli, started legal proceedings against her in the state of Uttar Pradesh for corrupt electoral practices after she defeated him in the 1971 elections. Early in June, 1975, Mrs. Gandhi was convicted on the charge in the Allahabad High Court, the state's highest judicial body, and the conviction gave further impetus to the agitation of students and workers, who began demanding her removal from office. On June 25th, she invoked an emergency constitutional provision concerning threats to national security, and sought, and obtained, from Fakhruddin Ali Ahmed, who was then the President of India (and, by the terms of the constitution, little more than a figurehead), a proclamation of what has been known ever since as the Emergency. Immediately following the President's proclamation, she rounded up and locked up without charges or trial thousands of her political opponents—including some of her father's venerable colleagues, such as Jaya Prakash Narayan, the seventy-two-year-old spiritual father of India. She curbed the press and the judiciary, suspended the constitution, and established a dictatorship. Mrs. Gandhi defended the Emergency after the fact by saying that she was ushering in a new era—what she called "the new India." Among her rationales for the suspension of the constitution was the impotence of the courts, which, she said, permitted wrongdoers who could afford expert lawyers to escape justice altogether. She pushed through an omnibus Forty-second Amendment, designed to strengthen the excutive at the expense of the courts and Parliament. She also used the Emergency to launch what she called a Twenty-Point Programme for economic development, with the stated aim of improving the lot of the poor. (This was immediately dismissed as a matter more of slogans than of serious economic policy.) It was generally thought that she had been reluctant to resort to the authoritarian Emergency, because it was contrary to the liberal principles of her father, and that Sanjay had persuaded her to do so. In any case, Sanjay became the Emergency's main beneficiary.

Propagandists of the Emergency began presenting Sanjay as a rising political leader; they compared him to the sun, the moon, and "the rising orbs," and hailed him as Messiah Sanjay. Although he held no political office and no position in the government, Mrs. Gandhi helped him assume an ever more important behind-the-scenes role in Congress Party politics, as a member of the executive committee of its youth wing. His mother was grooming him much as her father, consciously or otherwise, had groomed her, but at a greatly accelerated pace and despite the fact that Sanjay had clearly demonstrated a total lack of patience with the constitution and with democracy and was generally considered to be a spoiled, tyrannical child. In practice, he became almost as powerful as his mother. He quickly acquired his own set of *chamchas,* or spoons—in common Indian parlance, sycophants who would feed their leader as servants would feed a king, or as indulgent parents would feed their children. (Since most people in India eat with their fingers or go hungry, to be even someone else's spoon has a certain cachet.) He dictated orders in his mother's name to officials and politicians everywhere. He toured the various states as her chief emissary. (In time, he got himself a pilot's license and started piloting the planes he travelled in. On the road, he had gone in for speeding; in the air, he went in for daredevil stunts.) He inaugurated what he called a Four-Point Programme—of mass sterilization, slum clearance *cum* tree planting, abolition of dowries, and extension of literacy. Three of the points immediately met with popular protest: mass sterilization was seen as, among other things, an attack on the sanctity of the family, slum clearance as an attack on the sanctity of the home, and abolition of dowries as an attack on the sanctity of marriage. (Extending literacy had long been a government objective.) Moreover, the targets of these campaigns were the very poor and so the most defenseless; the method he and his supporters employed was often coercion; and the results were usually doubtful. (For instance, officials were so eager to swell the statistics of the mass-sterilization campaign that they sometimes sterilized healthy poor boys who had never been married.) Sanjay became the main symbol of the authoritarian Emergency.

For most of the Emergency, Mrs. Gandhi, it seemed, could not make up her mind whether she was, at heart, a liberal socialist democrat (a true child of Nehru) or a conservative aristocratic dictator (a true mother of Sanjay). Sometimes she talked as if the totalitarian means of the Emergency could be separated from the socialist ends she hoped to attain through them; at other times she talked as if she understood that ignoble means could not achieve noble ends. But at last she appeared to find a way of being true to the memory of her father while also pleasing her son: in January, 1977, she announced free and open Parliamentary elections to be held in March, released most of the political prisoners, and relaxed many of the authoritarian Emergency measures. She evidently felt confident that the elections would produce a mandate for her and Sanjay, legitimatizing the Emergency by once and for all disposing of the charge that it was a cloak for family dictatorship. Clearly, she was a victim of her own Emergency propaganda, for she never doubted that the mandate would be forthcoming. Sanjay, however, seemed to sense that there could be no halfway house to dictatorship, for he warned her against entrusting their joint future to the fickle electorate.

Mrs. Gandhi, in making her decision to hold elections, did not take into account either the power of Jaya Prakash Narayan or the possibility of defections from her own camp. Although Narayan was an agnostic socialist, in the minds of millions he had come to take the place of Mahatma Gandhi, the orthodox

man of God. Like Gandhi, he was deemed to be a disinterested
leader who cared only for the welfare of the nation. Some twenty
years earlier, he had renounced power and political ambition
for social service and the promotion of voluntary land reform
in the villages. He had no children. He had spent the early
months of the Emergency as a political prisoner, but then had
been released, because he suffered from a severe kidney disorder.
Now, though he was still ill, he inspired and encouraged all
the disparate major parties—the Socialist Party, the Bharatiya
Lok Dal, the Jana Sangh, and the Old Congress Party—to unite
in one Janata, or People's, Party, in order to rid the country of
"the dictatorship of mother and boy." The new Janata Party
was immediately strengthened by a major defection from Mrs.
Gandhi's camp: when the election campaign had barely started,
Jagjivan Ram—who was the leader of a hundred million Untouchables, had been in the Cabinet almost continuously since
Independence, and was probably Mrs. Gandhi's most important
Minister—denounced her and her Emergency, and founded the
Congress for Democracy, which at once joined forces with the
Janata Party. "The coming general elections provide perhaps
the last opportunity for preventing the total reversal of the nation's cherished policies, and for correcting the illegitimacy that
predominates in several aspects of our national life," he said
in his letter of resignation to Mrs. Gandhi, only to elicit from
her this reponse: "It is strange you should have remained silent
all these months, but should make these baseless charges now."
He did not bother to explain the reason for his change of heart;
some thought that he had got tired of the oppression of the
Emergency, which until the moment of his defection he had
helped to perpetuate, and others later decided that he had cun-
ningly sensed Mrs. Gandhi's approaching defeat and, being a
born opportunist, had abandoned her before the electorate could
abandon both of them.

If Jaya Prakash Narayan's role in founding the Janata Party

and Jagjivan Ram's defection were the two most important political events of the election campaign, its two overriding issues were the excesses of the mother, who would jail her father's friends and colleagues to enthrone her son, and the excesses of the son, who would stop at nothing—not even forced sterilization—to achieve his totalitarian ends. As the polling time approached, it began to look as if Mrs. Gandhi and Sanjay—who was standing for a Parliamentary seat for the first time, from Amethi, an Uttar Pradesh constituency neighboring his mother's Rae Bareli—and, indeed, their entire Congress Party might lose. Sanjay advised his mother to cancel the elections, on the ground that the opposition's campaigning was jeopardizing law and order—one of the grounds on which she had had the Emergency proclaimed. Either the advice came so late in the day that she feared she might have a revolution on her hands if she tried to abort the elections or her upbringing by her father proved so strong that it eclipsed her concern for both her own interests and her son's; in any event, she let the elections proceed.

On March 21, 1977, the election results were announced, and, in perhaps the greatest election upset anywhere at any time, Mrs. Gandhi and the Congress Party—the party that had ruled India for thirty years—were trounced at the polls. Out of five hundred and forty-two seats, the Janata Party and the Congress for Democracy together won two hundred and ninety-nine, while Mrs. Gandhi's Congress Party garnered only a hundred and fifty-three. (The other seats were dispersed among independents and members of sundry minor parties.) Both Mrs. Gandhi and Sanjay were badly defeated in their constituencies. Political commentators were so confounded by the results that they reached for metaphors like "the Janata wave" and "paternal disapproval from the beyond" to explain them, but it has since been generally held that the main reason for this great election upset was Sanjay, who had become the most hated man in India. (His campaign for forced sterilization, which involved mass vasectomies, was popularly confused with castration, and it spread fear through the countryside.)

In the aftermath of the elections, there were three main contenders for the Prime Ministership, each of whom led one of the parties in the Janata amalgam: sixty-eight-year-old Jagjivan Ram, the leader of the Congress for Democracy; eighty-one-year-old Morarji Desai, the leader of the Old Congress Party; and seventy-four-year-old Charan Singh, the leader of the Bharatiya Lok Dal, a left-of-center party with a following among independent small farmers. Both Desai and Charan Singh had spent most of the Emergency in jail. None of the three would defer to either of the others. It was thought that if the Janata members of the Parliament were to elect their leader democratically, the prize would go either to Jagjivan Ram or, more likely, to Charan Singh—for the Bharatiya Lok Dal had won the most seats. But Charan Singh was a regional leader from Uttar Pradesh, while Jagjivan Ram and Morarji Desai had national followings, and it was thought that neither of them would ever agree to take second place to Charan Singh. Even before the election results were widely known, the Janata Party seemed to be pulling apart, and, perhaps out of mixed motives of idealism and pragmatism, the three leaders finally agreed to let Jaya Prakash Narayan, aided by J. B. Kripalani, another elder statesman, name the next Prime Minister. This course caused some consternation among the Janata members of Parliament, who felt they had been elected on a platform of democracy and here, at the outset, were being made to bow to authoritarianism. On March 24th, Narayan tapped Desai—a taciturn elderly man who considered himself a follower of Mahatma Gandhi, though he was known for observing the letter rather than the spirit of the Mahatma's teachings—and Desai was thereupon sworn in as Prime Minister. He named Charan Singh his Minister of Home Affairs, a position second only to the Prime Ministership in power and influence.

The Janata, which ended thirty years of Congress Party rule of the central government, was immediately spoken of as a person in its own right. "It's Janata raj now," people said, or "It's Janata who now sits in Mrs. Gandhi's chair and gives orders." When the lights went off because of the power shortage, people cursed Janata, and when the lights went back on, people gave thanks to Janata. Desai's government was spoken about as if it were a Hindu god with many heads and more arms, the apotheosis of the Party's conflicting opinions and personalities.

People spoke of the Janata victory as "the wave," "the cyclone," "the wind." It was as if the victory defied ordinary political analysis and could no more be understood than natural phenomena could. A few months before the Emergency, people used to refer contemptuously to the poor as "dumb millions" or "ignorant masses," or simply as "the blight." Now that the Janata was in power, people referred to the same poor as "the true democrats," "the saviors," "the salt of the earth." The name of Lincoln was invoked in declarations that not all the poor can be fooled all the time. Astrologers were consulted to find out what the poor were thinking. Slogans and jingles, ballads and folk songs, ghoulish tales and morality playlets started weaving an oral tradition around the Emergency, as if it had been the reign of a villainous monarch.

In the first summer of Janata rule, politicians and officials were gossiping and tittering about a ten-thousand-word document that had been encased in steel and buried forty feet underground at the Red Fort, the Mogul monument in Delhi. The document was a time capsule that had been prepared by Mrs. Gandhi's government at a cost of thirty thousand rupees (four thousand dollars), and it contained an account of Indian history from Independence, on August 15, 1947, through August 15, 1972. It immortalized only seven people, and three of them turned out to be foreigners. In and out of Parliament, people asked "On whose authority was the capsule buried?" and "Where is the relevant file?" and "Who prepared the file?" and "Who decided which names to preserve for posterity?" P. C. Chunder, the new Janata Minister of Education, Social Welfare, and Culture, promised to launch an investigation, and to have the capsule dug up and its contents exposed. A professor named S. Krishnaswamy finally came forward and took responsibility for having provided the material for the time-capsule history. "The whole episode has now become so amusing that I feel tempted to write a history of this time capsule purely for its entertainment value," he wrote in a letter to the press. "I wish to mention, particularly for the sake of those who have an academic interest in the subject, that my emphasis in my teaching and writing of history has been on the significant socioeconomic movements of the people rather than on the achievements or failures of individual leaders. This is the reason why the omission of the names of several of our national leaders occurred in my version of the capsule history." The Red Fort capsule was one of three time capsules bequeathed by Mrs. Gandhi's government. Meanwhile, the Janata government announced that all the honorary titles that had been bestowed on distinguished citizens every year since Independence were forthwith revoked, because they were often unmerited and, furthermore, "unconstitutional." Anyone displaying his or her title on stationery, a calling card, or a signboard was to be prosecuted. The French sculptor Freda Brilliant, who had been working for many months on a Congress Party-commissioned seven-foot bronze statue of Mrs. Gandhi, was peremptorily informed by the new Janata government that her commission was cancelled. In 1976, a Hindu mother in the village of Karwar had named her son Sanjay. On July 25, 1977, which was the baby's birthday, she changed his name to Sanjiva, after Neelam Sanjiva Reddy, who on that day, under Janata auspices, assumed office as the new President of India.

The Janata government restored civil liberties and reëstablished a rule of law, helped to bolster the nation's democratic institutions, and gave the Indian political scene, for the first time, at least the appearance of a two-party system. But, leaving aside the period of the Emergency, the difference between the Congress Party and the Janata Party seemed, as time went on, to be one of style more than of substance, one of rhetoric more than of policy. During the election campaign, Janata politicians had presented themselves as austere and dedicated, in contrast to their Congress opponents, who were portrayed as self-indulgent and power-hungry. But, once victorious, Janata politicians lost no time in moving into the big government bungalows and offices of their predecessors and surrounding themselves with the customary retinue of servants and clerks. Similarly, during the election campaign the Janata Party had excoriated the Emergency laws and amendments, but it was quick to use them when doing so suited its purposes. It even resorted to the hated Emergency Forty-second Amendment to force elections in June, 1977, for the state legislatures—most of which were controlled by the Congress Party—on the ostensible ground that the legislatures' moral authority had been undermined by the Janata victory in the Parliamentary elections. As everybody had expected, the Janata Party was swept into power in most of the states.

The Janata had come to national power on a negative vote— a protest vote against the Emergency. It had neither a history nor an organization, neither an ideology nor a program, of its own. Most of its constituent parties had started out as splinter groups of the Congress Party, and on taking office the Janata immediately began encouraging large-scale defections from the Congress. The more the constituent parties tried to bury their past and change their identity in order to present a unified Janata front, the more they looked like the Congress. The Janata established sway over the whole country, but it stood on a patch of political quicksand.

Janata leaders often compared the Emergency with British

colonial rule and spoke of their overthrow of Mrs. Gandhi as "the second nonviolent revolution," the Congress overthrow of the British being the first. Like the Congress governments, the Janata government was right of center but awash with socialist rhetoric. This contrast between political reality and political rhetoric had its roots in the contradiction between, on the one hand, India's huge size and low per-capita income (ranked one hundred and ninth in the world) and, on the other, India's early Western-type industrialization and high gross national product (ranked ninth in the world). The Janata government, however—arguing that central planning had failed, because money and effort tended to be siphoned off into proliferating bureaucracy and regulations without ever reaching the villages—made it known that it would depart from the policies of the Congress government in at least one respect: it would deëmphasize the socialist concept of central planning for Western-type industrialization in favor of Mahatma Gandhi's concept of grass-roots schemes for small irrigation projects and cottage industries. With such schemes, the Janata government hoped to build a power base that was more solid than a protest vote, but there was no assurance that they would be more effective than central planning. Moreover, critics said, five or ten years later it might turn out that these schemes were impractical, and that central planning, with all its shortcomings, was the only practical approach for a poor country in the twentieth century.

The theoretical debate about central planning had barely got under way when it was pushed aside by the public's preoccupation with a series of "mother and boy" scandals, fostered by the new atmosphere of freedom. One night in July, 1977, a seventy-year-old widow, Mrs. Savitri Khanna, who worked as head housekeeper at one of the best hotels in New Delhi, the Oberoi Intercontinental, and who lived alone in one of the best sections of the city, Defense Colony, was found murdered in her bed—

strangled, with many knife wounds. The next day, wags said, "She used to provide Sanjay and his friends with girls and hotel rooms during the Emergency—they had to get rid of her," and "That's why they stabbed her so many times—they had to make sure she was really dead." The *Times of India,* a leading national English-language daily, noted in its story about the murder, "Among the visitors to her house today were Mr. Dinesh Singh, M.P. [at one time, Mrs. Gandhi's Minister of External Affairs], and Mr. Mohammed Yunus, former special envoy to Mrs. Indira Gandhi." In reality, the woman had retired from her job at the hotel in the early months of the Emergency, before Sanjay attained his enormous power; a former house servant and an accomplice were eventually arrested and charged with her murder, with the motive of robbery.

One day soon after Mrs. Khanna's murder, a man on a bicycle came out of a post office in New Delhi and was run over by a car. The capital was alive with more rumors: "Sanjay has had his cook killed" and "No, it was Sanjay's cook's son—he knew more than the cook" and "No, no, it was Sanjay's driver—he knew the most of all." In reality, the dead man had worked in some capacity in Mrs. Gandhi's house, but no one could find out what he knew, if anything.

Other scandals were even more elusive. Several Janata politicians produced evidence in Parliament that when Mrs. Gandhi realized that she might lose the election she had attempted to coerce the personal physician of Jagjivan Ram into getting the turncoat admitted to a hospital as a heart patient, so that he would be immobilized in the crucial last weeks of the campaign. Other Janata politicians charged that Mrs. Gandhi was responsible for the death, in February, of President Fakhruddin Ali Ahmed. They gave this scenario: Although she knew he was convalescing from a heart attack, she had rushed him back from Malaysia, where he had gone on a tour, and had then paid him a secret visit in the middle of the night, insisting that he cancel the elections and declare martial law. (According to this scenario, she knew as early as February that she had blundered—that her political life was in peril.) Fakhruddin Ali Ahmed had refused. She had ranted and raved at him. He had become so agitated that he suffered another heart attack and died.

In the early months of Janata rule, the *Statesman*, the *Times of India*, and the other two leading English-language dailies— the *Indian Express* and the *Hindustan Times*—and also the vernacular newspapers regularly published names and addresses of people who were tortured and killed during the Emergency, some of them on the personal orders of Sanjay, some by police officers trying to curry favor with the Gandhi family. But these reports, for all their air of authenticity, were hard to confirm. Likewise, printing presses regularly published pamphlets and tracts attacking Sanjay: "VIP Car Thief?" told of how teen-aged Sanjay had stolen and smashed a car, and portrayed him as an overgrown delinquent; "Maruti to Mafia" told of how Sanjay had established a huge factory just outside New Delhi to produce his Maruti and had then also used it as a front for criminal activities, and portrayed him as a Mafia figure. But such pamphlets and tracts only muddied the waters. Again, an investigative report in a local weekly claimed that on the night of Mrs. Gandhi's defeat one of Sanjay's emissaries plane-hopped from New Delhi to the Maldives and on to Sri Lanka, taking a circuitous route and returning within a week, so that his journey could not be traced or his absence noticed. The insinuation was that the agent was on a secret mission to put Sanjay's Emergency loot out of the reach of the Janata government. But the report was pieced together from doubtful airline-ticket and baggage records, and hence was more conjecture than fact. And, again, the *Statesman* splashed on its front page a photograph of a bank draft that it had obtained from an anonymous reader, purporting to show that Sanjay had transferred money to the account of his young wife, Maneka (formerly Menaka), in Switzerland. The photograph was published on the same day as the news of the military coup in Pakistan and all but overshadowed that event. The draft was immediately seized upon as documentary proof that Sanjay had huge sums of money hidden away in secret foreign accounts, and there were cries in Parliament for a full-fledged inquiry. After weeks of uproar, investigation, and representations to the Swiss government, the Janata government reluctantly concluded that the draft was a fake.

Many scandals of Mrs. Gandhi's Emergency regime seemed more tangible, however, perhaps because they became enmeshed in court proceedings. One case concerned the theft and destruction of a film satirizing Sanjay and Mrs. Gandhi and entitled "Kissa Kursi Ka" ("Tale of a Chair"). In July, 1975, Mrs. Gandhi's government had confiscated the negative and all the prints of the film, whereupon its producer, one Amrit Nahata, had petitioned the Supreme Court to get his film back, but the following November, eleven days before the film was scheduled to be screened in the Court, the confiscated material had mysteriously disappeared, leaving the producer without the film—the evidence for his petition. After the overthrow of Mrs. Gandhi, it was alleged that Sanjay, with R. K. Dhawan, private secretary to Mrs. Gandhi, and V. C. Shukla, her Minister for Information and Broadcasting, had burned the film in the sanctuary of Sanjay's car factory. Another case concerned Maruti, Ltd., which owned the car factory. Despite vast expenditures over many years, and continuous government support, Sanjay had managed to produce only a Maruti prototype—and that with imported parts—which he had exhibited to numerous dignitaries, including his mother, in New Delhi during the Emergency. He had not succeeded in producing a single roadworthy Maruti. After the overthrow of Mrs. Gandhi, Sanjay's shareholders and creditors had taken him to court, charging him with violating the terms of his license by designing a very expensive car, which contained many imported parts, and so squandering their investment. They had also charged Sanjay and the other directors with fraud and embezzlement. As a result, the car factory had been shut down, and liquidation proceedings had been instituted against the company. Still another case linked Sanjay to the murder of a dacoit named Sunder, sung and celebrated as a local Robin Hood. The story ran that Sanjay and Sunder had been chums but had fallen out over—among other things—Sanjay's mass-vasectomy program. Sunder had seen the program as an affront to the poor and had addressed several threatening letters to Sanjay, swearing that he would avenge the suffering of the poor with Sanjay's blood. Soon afterward, he had been arrested, and the two had met in public. Sanjay, a self-styled near-monarch, had slapped Sunder, and Sunder, a handcuffed prisoner, had spat in Sanjay's face. It was alleged that Sanjay had shortly had Sunder bound, gagged, and drowned in the night.

Perhaps the most scandalous rumor concerned the shooting death of Sanjay's father-in-law, Lieutenant Colonel T. S. Anand, early in June, 1977. Some said that it had been murder, others that it had been suicide. Proponents of the murder theory maintained that Sanjay had had his father-in-law killed, because he was the weak link in Sanjay's defense in his various court cases, while proponents of the suicide theory maintained that the Colonel had been so depressed by his knowledge of Sanjay's crimes that he did himself in. The arguments for either theory remained inconclusive, not least because the murder or suicide weapon was never found. Under the headline "DEAD MEN TELL NO TALES," a story in *India Today*—a local English-language fortnightly that aspired to the journalism of American news weeklies—cited a few known facts and set out the arguments favoring each theory:

> The fact: The body was lying in the open for two days and yet seemed to have been left untouched by vultures, dogs etc.

33

In favour of murder: The deduction could be that Col. Anand was shot dead somewhere else and his body brought and carefully placed in the open field.

In favour of suicide: Police say that there have been incidents when the body has lain outside for ten days without being touched by vultures.

The fact: The position of the body was a little too neat, with hands by the side and the legs straight out.

In favour of murder: The possibility that the body was laid out in the position after the murder had been committed.

In favour of suicide: There have been instances when the hand drops to the side. The fact that forensic experts have said that he was shot in a prone position could be interpreted to mean that he had first lain down and then shot himself.

The fact: There were three newspapers and an empty carton usually meant to carry batteries in which some "heavy object" was carried.

In favour of suicide: That Col. Anand carried the revolver in the empty carton and, depressed by reading the newspapers all of which carried stories about Sanjay and his misdeeds, shot himself.

In favour of murder: The three newspapers were old issues and one of them had been given to Col. Anand to fan himself. It is improbable that Col. Anand had not been following the charges against Sanjay in the press every day. Further there is no evidence to show that Col. Anand had carried or carries his firearms with him.

The fact: A small note identified as being written by Col. Anand which said: "Sanjay worry unbearable."

In favour of suicide: That this was a suicide note.

In favour of murder: That with his army background Col. Anand would have written a far fuller note. If he was meticulous enough to spread out newspapers beneath his head, lie down in a rigid position before shooting himself he would definitely have written a full suicide note.

The fact: There were no signs of struggle and the blood trickle showed that it was a clean shot.

In favour of suicide: Forensic reports that the lack of struggle and the nature of the wound would point to suicide.

Conclusion: In the seesaw tussle between the murder and suicide theories what perhaps has been overlooked is that the possibility of murder cannot be overlooked even if all the evidence points to suicide. The police have not given any clue as to the details of the post-mortem but there is a possibility that Col. Anand was drugged and then shot at point-blank range. In the case of drugging, the position of body, the nature of the wound, the apparent absence of any sign of struggle could all be explained.

Whether it is suicide or murder by drugging, the police eagerness to write it off as suicide seems to be a little surprising. What is wanted is a thorough probe—and for once not by the blundering Delhi Police.

Other rumors and charges in the press, Parliament, and the courts implicated Mrs. Gandhi herself in crimes. It was said, for instance, that her cupboards used to "burst open with packets of hundred-rupee notes," and that she had smuggled some Congress Party money abroad as a "nest egg." But the most bizarre case concerned what came to be generally known as the Nagarwala affair. On the morning of May 24, 1971, one V. P. Malhotra, chief cashier of the Parliament Street branch of the State Bank of India, in New Delhi, had supposedly received a telephone call from Prime Minister Indira Gandhi, who told him that she had an urgent need for money. Malhotra had then taken six million rupees in hundred-rupee notes from the bank vault, put the money in a trunk, loaded the trunk into a staff car, and driven away. At an appointed place, he had met one Rustom Sohrab Nagarwala. Malhotra had asked him, *"Aap kis desh ka babuji—bharat ka?"* ("You are from what country, sir—from

India?''), whereupon Nagarwala had replied, *"Mai Bangla Desh ka, babuji"* ("I am from Bangladesh, sir"). This exchange of previously agreed-upon passwords had identified Nagarwala as Mrs. Gandhi's emissary, and Malhotra had turned the trunk over to him. Following Nagarwala's instructions, Malhotra had appeared at Mrs. Gandhi's residence for a receipt, but had failed to get it or to see her. He had then gone to a police station and reported that he had been the victim of a fraud. By nightfall, police had arrested Nagarwala and recovered almost all the money. In due course, Nagarwala had confessed to having duped Malhotra by imitating Mrs. Gandhi's voice on the telephone. The affair had become a topic of discussion in Parliament, where some opposition members alleged that Mrs. Gandhi was keeping a secret account in the State Bank for Party and personal use. But at the time Mrs. Gandhi had been almost at the peak of her power; the case had been quickly disposed of and the affair silenced. Subsequently, Nagarwala had died in jail, and the officer in charge of the investigation had been killed in a road accident. In 1977, six years after the embezzlement, the affair became a subject of Janata inquiry, like everything else connected with mother and son and the Emergency.

2

Fathers and Sons

Desai's Janata government came to office amid hopeful and idealistic pronouncements, but Desai and Charan Singh immediately clashed over what to do about Mrs. Gandhi and Sanjay. Mrs. Gandhi had served as Prime Minister for eleven years; she was the only truly national figure in politics. The question being asked was "Will she be arrested and tried?" Many people were convinced that she had committed Watergate-type crimes during the Emergency. Some were anticipating and some dreading that the police would escort her to jail. Many felt that not to hold her accountable—and thus punishable—for those supposed crimes was, of course, inequitable, but also felt that no matter how carefully the Janata government might develop its case against her, no matter how solid its evidence against her might be, her arrest and trial would smack of political vengeance and might prepare the way for her return to office. The Janata leaders immediately recognized that she posed a formidable threat to their government.

Charan Singh, heading a group who became known as hawks, agitated for a speedy, Nuremberg-type trial of Mrs. Gandhi, Sanjay, and their associates—like V. C. Shukla and Bansi Lal, the Defense Minister during the Emergency—who had come to be dubbed the Sanjay Caucus, or merely the Caucus. Desai headed the so-called doves, who wanted to establish several commissions of inquiry, in order first to expose and publicize the "crimes and horrors of the Emergency" and then to let the mother, the son, and the Caucus be tried, like other citizens, in the ordinary courts. The hawks argued that the Indian judicial system was notorious for its slow, almost endless procedures, and consequently the Emergency criminals could circumvent justice through endless appeals. (Ironically, they were resorting to one of Mrs. Gandhi's rationales for the Emergency.) The doves argued that the Janata Party had won at the polls precisely by promising to restore, among other things, the integrity of the judiciary, and that any hint of peremptory proceedings against the very people who had traduced that integrity would belie the Janata cause; moreover, said the doves, jail would make martyrs of mother and son. (Since British times, jail has conferred a special status on politicians, and has been the surest road to political power—as the Janata victory itself demonstrated.) Charan Singh belonged to the subcaste of Jats, from Uttar Pradesh, and lived up to the Jats' reputation—of being impetuous and vengeful people, who seek swift personal justice. Similarly, Desai, who came from the state of Gujarat, upheld the Gujaratis' reputation—of being patient and tenacious people, who slowly tie their adversaries hand and foot in a spiderweb of legal complications that ultimately bankrupt them. Thus, the hawks and the doves in the Cabinet were soon locked in a hopeless struggle.

The 1952 Act of the Commissions of Inquiry gave the government the right to establish commissions that would have the power to subpoena people and documents, much as law courts do, and in April, 1977, the Janata government appointed Jayantilal C. Shah, a retired Chief Justice of the Supreme Court, as a one-man commission to investigate "all complaints of excesses, malpractices, and abuses of authority" on the part of Mrs. Gandhi, Sanjay, and their associates. The commission was given a mandate to investigate, among other things, forced sterilization of the urban poor and their relocation, and arrests of political prisoners and their maltreatment.

On September 29th, the Shah Commission began much-publicized hearings—calling witnesses and taking testimony, exhibiting documents and reading them into the record. It seemed that every day the commission ferreted out new scandals about the Emergency; that every day the government reacted with fresh statements of condemnation or created more commissions of inquiry. "There is no parallel to this inquiry in all the previous inquiries held by the Central and State Governments in India," a press release from Charan Singh's Ministry of Home Affairs observed. "In fact, there is no parallel to this inquiry even as regards inquiries held by similar Commissions or Tribunals in the United States, U.K., etc. . . . The scope of this inquiry is truly gigantic in nature." Other commissions, fact-finding committees, departmental bodies started inquiring specifically into riots over Sanjay's forced-sterilization policy in Delhi's Turkman Gate area in April, 1976; into allegations of corruption against Bansi Lal and other members of the Caucus; and so on. During the Emergency, Maruti, Ltd., though it had not succeeded in producing a roadworthy car, had grown into many affiliated Maruti concerns—Maruti Heavy Vehicles Private, Ltd., Maruti Technical Services, Ltd., and others. The commission empanelled to investigate this group of companies aroused the most public interest, possibly because Sanjay's obsession with his Maruti was considered one of the underlying causes of Mrs. Gandhi's downfall. The commission was to examine why and how Sanjay had received a government monopoly to produce his notorious car: Had the directors of Maruti, Ltd., violated any laws in acquiring land for their car factory; in raising capital; in pressuring car dealers to order Maruti cars; in financial dealings with friends, relatives, and dependents; in obtaining scarce, controlled commodities like steel and cement; in profiting from foreign-exchange transactions with foreign collaborators? The Janata government filed a series of suits charging Sanjay and other directors of at least three of the Maruti concerns with corruption. The government alleged in one suit that the directors of Maruti, Ltd., had conspired with the officials of the Delhi Transport Corporation to receive overpayment, to the tune of a hundred and twenty thousand rupees, for some Maruti buses. The government alleged in another suit that the directors of Maruti Heavy Vehicles Private, Ltd., had conspired with officials of the Oil and Natural Gas Commission, and had supplied the commission with defective road rollers, even passing off as new Maruti equipment some old, unserviceable rollers manufactured by another firm. The government alleged in still another suit that the directors of Maruti Technical Services, Ltd., in collusion with the officials of the Municipal Corporation of Delhi, had fraudulently obtained a contract worth two million one hundred thousand rupees to sell the municipality a chemical called Quick Floc Polymix for the treatment of the municipal water supply, with full knowledge that the chemical might be toxic.

The progress of the various inquiries and cases soon bogged down, however, because officials said that not enough men of stature could be found in the country to sit on the various panels. Some well-known candidates disqualified themselves because of conflict of interest or because of an appearance of partiality. Others, eager to serve, were disqualified by having played chameleonlike roles during and following the Emergency. Thus, after half a dozen justices and ex-justices had declined to head the commission to investigate the group of Maruti companies, D. S. Mathur, a retired Chief Justice of the Allahabad High Court, was prevailed upon to accept the task. Mathur was considered a good choice because in 1971 he had been instrumental in the appointment to the Allahabad High Court of the justice Jag Mohan Lal Sinha, who four years later gave the judgment against Mrs. Gandhi in the renowned Rae Bareli election case.

But Mathur's inquiry had hardly got under way when Justice Sinha, his old protégé, charged him with being partial to the Gandhi family. Sinha claimed that Mathur had tried to influence Sinha's decision in the Rae Bareli election case by calling on him after dark with a message from Mrs. Gandhi and saying, "It is settled that today you decide the case in favour of [Mrs.] Gandhi and tomorrow you go to the Supreme Court." Justice Mathur was soon engulfed in a scandal of his own, and he immediately stepped down from the commission, declaring in his letter of resignation:

> I retired as Chief Justice of the Allahabad High Court in 1974 with an unblemished 38 years' record as magistrate and judge, happy in the regard and respect of the bench and the bar for whatever I was able to do to uphold the independence, integrity, and dignity of the judiciary. I had not expected this record to be sought to be tarnished when I came out of retirement to try and help a national cause by accepting the inquiry commission.
>
> The entire manner in which insinuations against me have been made deserves thorough investigation. I believe it will be in the public interest to have an investigation made.

So it was that before Emergency inquiries could get very far there had to be other inquiries, and no one could say where the process of inquiry would end.

The Janata government had meanwhile arrested, on Independence Day, in August, 1977, ten of Mrs. Gandhi's associates, among them her private secretary, Dhawan, and Dhawan's brother and his father; Yashpal Kapoor, the manager of Mrs. Gandhi's 1971 election campaign, whose political activities had led to Sinha's judgment against Mrs. Gandhi; and P. C. Sethi, the treasurer of the Congress Party and Mrs. Gandhi's Minister of Chemicals and Fertilizers. These arrests had been followed within a few days by that of Bansi Lal, perhaps Sanjay's closest associate. Dhawan, Kapoor, Sethi, and Lal (together with Shukla, Pranab Mukerjee, and Om Mehta) had formed the Sanjay Caucus, which, it was generally accepted, had practically ruled the country during much of the Emergency. They all stood charged with siphoning off Congress Party funds into bogus companies and from there into their own pockets. Among subsequent arrests were those of H. R. Gokhale, Mrs. Gandhi's Minister of Law; K. D. Malviya, her Minister of Petroleum; and D. P. Chattopadhyaya, her Minister of Commerce. During all this, Sanjay seemed to be shuttling from one investigative body or court to another in an effort to extricate himself from a web of cases, in which he stood accused of conspiracy, of blackmail, of torture, and of involvement in the murder of Sunder. Every day, the newspapers were filled with nothing but the crimes of the Emergency—of Mrs. Gandhi, her Ministers, her son. Mrs. Gandhi came to dominate the news and the doings of the government to such an extent that she became, in effect, the ruler in absentia.

There were many people outside the Janata government who felt that it should get on with the job of governing, and leave Mrs. Gandhi to the newspapers and the history books. They pointed to the legal concept sometimes referred to as "the reason of state," which allows an exception to the principle that all are equal before the law, the exception being that if the trial of a deposed head of state would be more injurious to the commonweal than no trial this principle may be suspended.

While the issue of the speedy trial continued to be debated in the Cabinet, it fell to Charan Singh, the hawk, as Minister of Home Affairs, to carry out the dove policy and prepare a case against Mrs. Gandhi for prosecution in the ordinary courts. On October 3, 1977, he had Mrs. Gandhi, along with several members of the Caucus, arrested on charges that she had coerced two Indian companies into donating a hundred and fourteen jeeps for the Congress Party's use in the campaign for the March Parliamentary elections—and had then refurbished the jeeps and sold them to the Army as new equipment—and that she had conspired to award a government contract to a French oil company whose bid was twelve million dollars higher than the bid of an American oil company. Although Charan Singh claimed that his case was "iron-clad," its initial presentation was so clumsy and incompetent that the municipal magistrate who heard the case dismissed it for lack of evidence and unconditionally released Mrs. Gandhi. Charan Singh immediately had the decision appealed, but the arrest had thrown into doubt the Janata government's motives for proceeding against her in the first place. Charan Singh may have been goaded into action by events in Pakistan, where former Prime Minister Zulfikar Ali Bhutto had been arraigned for conspiracy to murder a political opponent, or by Mrs. Gandhi's ever more strident criticisms of the Janata leaders in her ever more numerous speaking tours through the country, or by a wish to divert attention from the Janata's increasingly apparent inability to deal quickly with India's huge problems. Whatever the reason (or reasons), by the largely symbolic act of arresting her the government helped to resurrect Mrs. Gandhi politically from the ashes of the Emergency.

Charan Singh was pilloried in the press and the Parliament. His case was so ill prepared, it was said, and the charges he had brought were so minor compared with the daily revelations of Mrs. Gandhi's abuse of power that the proceedings were a travesty of justice. If he could botch such an important case, how could he expect to run a whole department, let alone the country? It was said in his defense, however, that though he got the blame, he had actually done an unintended service in exposing the futility of the dovish policy of minor, piecemeal law actions that could be stymied anywhere along the legal road by the caprice of a hearing magistrate or by a maze of technicalities. Anyway, not only Mrs. Gandhi but Sanjay and all Mrs. Gandhi's Ministers were free pending their trials. It was recalled that their arrests had been in defiance of the spirit of the Janata government's own inquiries, not to mention its leaders' witness that jail in India confers martyrdom and thereby becomes a route to high public office. It was also recalled that in the March Parliamentary election a trade-union leader named George Fernandes had stood for Parliament from jail and won. At the time, there had been serious criminal charges pending against him, such as using violence to overthrow the Emergency government, and he had been on his way to being convicted of the charges, but after Mrs. Gandhi's fall the Janata government had summarily dismissed them and had made him Minister of Industry. Who could say how the wheel of political fortune would turn?

In the family setting of Indian politics, where every issue is personalized, Charan Singh's supposed disgrace was interpreted as a triumph not only for Mrs. Gandhi but also for Desai. Charan Singh started pressing Desai to impanel an independent commission of inquiry to investigate the growing power and influence of Desai's own son, Kantilal. Kantilal, who was fifty-one years old, had been a target of charges of corruption; he was living with his father in the Prime Minister's residence, as Mrs. Gandhi and Sanjay had done with their respective parents. The demand for a commission of inquiry was tantamount to a demand for a trial of Kantilal. Charan Singh's detractors said that he was simply trying to embarrass Desai, in order to recoup the recent loss to his own prestige; his admirers said that he sincerely cared for good, clean government and wanted to dispel the growing impression that the only purpose the elections had served was to substitute the corrupt rule of a father and son for the corrupt rule of a mother and son. Whatever Charan Singh's motives, Desai must have found it galling for Kantilal, who had never taken part in politics, to be compared with Sanjay. Meanwhile, Charan Singh either prompted or allowed his supporters to plan a rally in the capital to celebrate his seventy-fifth birthday. On the appointed day—December 23, 1977—at least a million and a half independent small farmers, who were part of his political constituency of Jats, trooped into New Delhi from the neighboring states, giving the city a seething atmosphere that suggested a pending coup d'état. The rally itself was an innocuous affair, with speeches of felicitation and welcome, but no politician had ever held such a rally in the capital before, and it was seen as a show of personal force, intended to put Desai on notice that Charan Singh could not be discounted with impunity.

When Desai was asked about the rally, which he had declined to attend, he said he would not "join such things," because he did not approve of them. Charan Singh felt slighted, and later observed of Desai, "He did not care to consider that such an unsolicited statement would wound the feelings of his senior-most colleague. But then he was the Prime Minister, and I, a humble individual whom he could make or unmake. Few people would believe when I tell them that . . . Desai had not even the courtesy to felicitate me." He read portentous significance into Desai's absence, calling it indicative of his lack of interest in the peasantry. Later, Charan Singh gave on the floor of the Parliament his version of Desai's attitude toward the peasants: "The wretches living remote from the Capital are not within our ken. Nor do they seem to belong to us. They are denizens of a different world—uncouth and unlettered. What are the poverty-stricken people in the villages or even the towns to us, and we to them, that we should weep for them!"

Desai presided over a faction-ridden government, held together only by the realization that the departure of one faction, or even one leader, could bring the whole edifice down, and that its fall could precipitate an election that might bring back Mrs. Gandhi. The Janata government was faltering so badly that there were already signs of nostalgia for Mrs. Gandhi's rule, and her adversaries knew that the next time they would not be given a chance to campaign against her and put her in the dock. But on January 3, 1978, the Congress Party split over the issue of Mrs. Gandhi's continued leadership, and many of her long-standing colleagues, who had helped her rule during the Emergency and supported her even after the 1977 elections, ousted her and her followers from what they now began calling the Official Congress Party. She took refuge in a splinter party—soon named Congress Indira—and became its president, but there was no hiding the fact that she was left with a mere rump group. Then, on January 11th, she appeared before the Shah Commission under summons. She had been called many times before to testify but had refused even to appear. Now she refused to testify, charging that the commission's proceedings were a form of vendetta, and presenting herself as a persecuted politician whose only crime was that she had been true to her principles. She even condemned the Janata government for having caused an "alarming erosion in civil liberties." In actuality, she was condemning the commission in much the same terms as those in which the Janata leaders had condemned the Emergency while it was in force. Yet her sweeping claims could not conceal the fact that, with the indictment, she was politically all but finished, and the decline in her fortunes had the effect of strengthening Charan Singh's political hand: it now appeared likely that the fall of Desai's government would mean not Mrs. Gandhi's return but only the replacement of Desai by someone else. Desai was clearly as alert to the change in the political realities as Charan Singh, for on January 15th he announced at a rally that he would resign if any of the allegations against Kantilal were supported by prima-facie evidence—at the same time being careful to insinuate that such evidence was nonexistent, by calling the allegations "unfounded and mischievous." If he had hoped by his statement to put an end to demands for a commission of inquiry to investigate Kantilal, his hope was not realized. On March 11th, Charan Singh wrote him a letter (which he subsequently read into the Parliamentary record, along with many of their other exchanges) stating:

Shri Kantibhai Desai ["shri" is equivalent to "sir," and "bhai" to "brother"] is your only son and lives with you. Perhaps, as stated by you on the floor of the Parliament, you have appointed him as your Private Secretary also. . . .

People in general and publicmen in particular have, however, been disturbed to know that you do not propose to hold any enquiry at all. . . . Nevertheless, an enquiry would be appropriate. The reason is simple: every minister, much more so the Prime Minister along with such members of his family as are living jointly with him, should not only be incorruptible but should appear to be so.

Desai replied with a letter, dated March 13th, that said:

Some persons had been telling me that you were intending to write such a letter. . . .

Our country has somehow become a vast whispering gallery in which character assassination seems to be a pastime or a child's play and rumors seem to float as if they are facts. . . .

It has . . . become a fashion not only to involve Ministers but also their families in vague insinuations unworthy of any credence.

You will recall that there were so many persons insinuating about your son-in-law [*sic*] and without referring to you I defended him in Parliament because I refused to believe them. I have had a number of letters making allegations about you and your sons-in-law, and, painful to state, even your wife. . . . If we were to follow the principles you have mentioned in your letter to the logical conclusions we would be appointing a number of Commissions of Inquiry every day.

[Kantilal] has made it clear that as Private Secretary he does not deal with any official matters. He works virtually as Private Secretary to me in my personal, political (nonofficial) or domestic matters.

47

. . . In the circumstances any allegations and insinuations that he dabbles with official matters or there is a "Kanti Caucus" or "Kanti Junta" are mere figments of a wild imagination beneath notice. . . .

The Commissions that have already been appointed to look into the misdeeds of the previous regime and important functionaries in that regime is ample evidence of our keenness to curb this malady.

Charan Singh had five sons-in-law—one of them a member of the legislative assembly in Uttar Pradesh, another a sugar commissioner in that state, and a third a doctor in Delhi, while two lived abroad. At one time or another, the sugar commissioner and the doctor figured in scandals involving charges of corruption and medical malpractice. Certainly the references to the allegations against Charan Singh's sons-in-law and his wife could not have been calculated to calm the waters, even if Desai did point out that he gave them no credence. Charan Singh's response, dated March 21st, stated:

It is obvious that my letter has caused you some irritation—even anger. For, if it is not anger, how else is one expected to understand your reaction which, in essence, amounts to this: "If there are charges against my son, there are charges against your sons-in-law and wife too.". . .

Well, if there are charges against my relations and they reflect adversely on my integrity, they must be enquired into—*the sooner the better.* I would like you to kindly appoint a Commission at the earliest. It is precisely my point that any cover-up of such matters leads to contrary results. . . .

Inasmuch, however, as we are not willing to apply the same standards to ourselves, the appointment of Commissions "to look into the misdeeds of the previous regime" is no evidence that we are really keen to root out corruption. . . .

Now, political affairs of a Prime Minister in connection whereof Shri Kanti Desai, as he himself has put it, "meets and discusses things with political leaders and others" cannot be characterized as a purely private or personal, non-official or domestic matter. . . .

Further, Shri Kanti Desai is a member of a joint Hindu family with you as its head. Which means the financial interests of you both are the same. Legally this position leads to conclusions which are obvious. . . .

Your own good name and that of the country demand that a Commission is appointed.

It was now Desai's turn, and on March 23rd he replied:

There was no equation in my mind between Kanti's case and the case of your sons-in-law and your wife. I am not the one to look for alibis of this nature. . . .

Regarding Kanti's status, I think you are quite wrong in your analysis. There is no question of joint family being involved. He and I have separate identities; we are separately assessed; we may live under the same roof but have separate life of our own. He has his own affairs to look after and I have mine. If he meets and discusses things with political leaders and others it is mostly on their approach. They see him on organisational and such other non-official matters and mostly unasked. Should he say, "No," when they do so? I myself have tried to dissuade them from seeing him but they persist. In any case, if he deals with political matters, it is not possible for him to be restricted from seeing those who wish to see him or whom he has to see for non-official or personal matters.

I thank you for being so solicitous about my good name [and] that of the country. I can assure you that both are and will be safe in my own keeping and the day I am convinced that I cannot look after both, I have already told you what would be my line of action.

49

Charan Singh had his own reasons for raising the Kantilal problem, and Desai had his own reasons for denying it. But soon even Desai's admirers had to admit that the parallels between Kantilal and Sanjay were too striking to be ignored. Desai soon had his own "Sanjay problem" in Kantilal. Like Sanjay, Kantilal was a businessman. (He used to manufacture industrial magnets, but some years earlier he had sold the company and started working as his father's private secretary. He had a family of his own, but since then his wife and children had lived elsewhere.) Like Sanjay, Kantilal had never held any public office, had no official position, and acted as his parent's confidant. After Desai became Prime Minister, Kantilal started appearing with him at public rallies, diplomatic receptions, and press conferences. In June, 1977, he travelled with his father to the Commonwealth Prime Ministers' Conference in London, and soon afterward he accompanied his father on a political fence-mending trip to Kashmir. Like Sanjay, Kantilal was one of the main doorkeepers at the Prime Minister's office and home. Again like Sanjay, there was a touch of scandal about Kantilal. (In 1970, it was said, he had been caught with smuggled gold, and the case had apparently been hushed up.) A reporter for the *Statesman,* the paper that had done more than any other Indian paper to expose the influence of Sanjay on Mrs. Gandhi, had once tackled Desai on the subject of his son. Desai had replied:

> You know I am 81 and I do need help. What's wrong with it if my son helps me? . . . Are you telling me my son is a Sanjay Gandhi? . . . I know people talk about him, but I also know that he will not do any wrong. If you can cite one instance of wrongdoing in his part since I assumed office, I assure you I shall take action; I shall not even hesitate to resign. . . . What can I do if, among others, even journalists sometimes approach him . . . for interviews with me? He, of course, wards them off and he knows, too, that even if he speaks to me I would not do it. . . . Some people

write to me about it sometimes and I show these letters to him to let him know what people think. He understands. And as you would have seen, he is keeping as much in the background as possible.

Mrs. Gandhi, following the fall of her government, had withdrawn from public life for a time, but gradually and methodically she came out of her seclusion, increasingly conducting herself as though the Emergency had not happened, or, at least, as though its aberrations—just as some of her apologists charged—had been the fault of her zealous Ministers and advisers, and perpetrated without her knowledge. She began to talk as if she were still the leader of the Congress Party. For instance, in April, 1977, scarcely three weeks after the elections, she sent this open letter to D. K. Borooah, the retiring Congress president, to be circulated among the members of the Congress Working Committee:

> It is a matter of sorrow for all of us that the Congress has lost the battle of the ballot. But it is good that the change from one Government to the other has been peaceful and orderly. We respectfully bow to the verdict of the people and we wish the new Government stability and success in the service of the people. We always give first priority to the interests of the country. As we have already indicated we shall extend our coöperation to the Government for programmes for the welfare of the people. . . .
> So far as I am concerned I should like to make it clear that as one who led the Government, I unreservedly own full responsibility for this defeat. I am not interested in finding alibis or excuses for myself, nor am I interested in shielding anyone. I have no caucus to defend or group to fight. I have never functioned as a faction leader.
> This is a moment for introspection by each one of us. We have shared days of joy and sorrow. The Congress has

had trials and tribulations but it has also reached historic heights, both in the pre- and post-independence periods. The Congress has made an impact not only in India, but in one way or the other all over the world. It has striking achievements to its credit in the economic, scientific and international spheres. The economy was put on a sound basis and brought to a point where it was poised for rapid growth. A time may come when a more objective appreciation in this regard will be made even by those who are our critics today.

It is true that we failed to carry conviction with the people in winning a majority. Yet, if I may say so with utmost humility, even now the Congress remains the only organized national party existing in all parts of our country. It has a crucial role to play at this critical moment in Indian history. Those who have voted for it and those who have voted it out have many hopes and expectations from the Congress and the Congress cannot disappoint them. [Hundreds of thousands] of Congress workers all over the country are ready to face the new situation bravely. We must come closer to them and encourage their determination. . . .

The people of India have given me warm, unbounded love and affection over the years. With the assistance of my colleagues, I tried to serve them as best and as honestly as I could. I am aware of the anger with which they have voted us out. I own responsibility for this. During my election meetings and elsewhere, I have expressed my sorrow for any hardship or harassment which they experienced in the implementation of some of our programmes. We must all learn lessons from the past and be prepared to face the future and the consequences of our action. I shall continue to serve the people.

Everyone had expected the Congress Party to repudiate Mrs. Gandhi's leadership, but the letter had its intended mollifying effect. Then, on May 5th, when the All-India Congress Working

Committee met in New Delhi to elect a new president, she paid a surprise visit and spoke to the members penitently, at one point breaking into tears. Those assembled had never seen her cry before, and they were overwhelmed. Despite objections from a few dissidents, they promptly rubber-stamped her choice of K. Brahmananda Reddy as the new Congress president, although he had been the nominal Home Affairs Minister during the Emergency, and so, technically, responsible for its excesses. The columnist S. Nihal Singh commented in the *Statesman:*

> Mrs. Gandhi proffered the merest nod of imperious acceptance of responsibility without repudiating any of her own or her son's actions. The other leaders were faced with the problem of how a party of guilty men should act. Each one of them had aided or abetted Mrs. Gandhi in the Emergency, and lesser Congressmen had at the very least acquiesced. By choosing to blame "aberrations" and "deviations" and the "caucus" for the unspeakable crimes committed and the degradation to which the country was subjected, the dissidents had lost the battle even before challenging Mrs. Gandhi's nominee for the party's presidency. . . .
>
> Having been schooled in double-think during the Emergency, the leaders of the Congress Party have refused to be honest with the people in analyzing the enormity of their individual and collective guilt in promoting what a foreign observer aptly described as vegetarian fascism.

After Mrs. Gandhi's successful visit to the Congress Working Committee, she began making a growing number of carefully planned, well-timed appearances. She would drop by at embassies to help celebrate national days, and stay long enough to be seen—without, however, saying anything. But around the middle of July she seized the political initiative, and it happened that the opportunity to do so was given her by Charan Singh. On July

13th, Charan Singh had made a speech in Parliament in which he levelled a celebrated charge that Mrs. Gandhi's government had been "thinking" of liquidating the opposition leaders she had jailed during the Emergency. He had said that therefore there could be no question of "forgive and forget." The government was not a body of holy men, and it was irrelevant whether the guilty person was "he" or "she"—an indirect reference, of course, to Mrs. Gandhi. Charan Singh had offered only one piece of evidence for his "liquidation" charge: a statement in the Supreme Court during the Emergency by Mrs. Gandhi's Attorney General, Niren De, claiming that, in theory, the Emergency ordinance suspended all rights to a citizen and empowered the government to imprison anyone if it liked, to starve any prisoner if it liked, even to kill him, and there could be no remedy in the courts. (In De's words, "no one could claim the right to live.") The Congress members on the opposition benches had been stung by Charan Singh's charge. The next day, he had repeated it, and they had asked him to withdraw it immediately unless he could produce evidence. But then they had sensed that he had given them a real political issue, and they had staged a walkout from Parliament, crying that all the Janata government's apparatus of commissions and legal proceedings was only a smoke screen for the government's true intention of exacting a primitive, peasant revenge from mother and son. The Congress members had recalled that Charan Singh—the Emergency political prisoner—was from peasant stock and was an old Nehru-family foe. So it was that Charan Singh provided Mrs. Gandhi with her opportunity to make political hay. She issued this public statement:

> Since the last [Parliamentary] elections, when in all humility I accepted the full responsibility for the heavy reverses suffered by my party, the Congress, in the northern States,

I deliberately decided to keep away from politics and from personal and press publicity.

The institution of various commissions, covering a wide range of activities connected with my period in office, had led to the expectation that the law would be allowed to take its course.

However, I find that some leaders of the Janata Party Government are determined to pursue their smear campaign of character assassination inside and outside Parliament so as to denigrate not only me but the Congress Party as a whole. The Home Minister's recent statement about an alleged plan (or "thinking") in my Government to shoot down leaders of the Opposition in jail is shocking and preposterous and has no basis whatsoever. This is the very limit in malicious propaganda deliberately carried on by some leaders of the Janata Party. It is difficult to see how any one could rationally jump to such a wild conclusion on the basis of the theoretical and hypothetical arguments advanced by Mr. Niren De in the Supreme Court. . . . Nothing of this nature was remotely contemplated. The whole idea is outrageous and could occur only to one who himself thinks along these lines. It is one more instance of the type of misrepresentation and insinuation which are current these days. In fact, Mr. Jaya Prakash Narayan, Mr. [Atal Behari] Vajpayee, Mr. Charan Singh himself and other prominent leaders were allowed out on parole [during the Emergency] on information of ill-health.

That we believe in democracy is borne out by the fact that we took the major decision of holding elections which gave our people the opportunity of expressing their views and having a Government of their choice. . . .

I hope that the leaders of the Janata Party will at least now address themselves to the more serious and mounting problems affecting different sections of the people, especially industrial labour, farmers, the rural and urban poor, the minorities, the weaker sections and the middle classes. Imme-

diate attention has to be given to the atrocities on [Untoucha-
bles], increasing lawlessness and spiralling prices.

Mrs. Gandhi's critics saw her public statement as an audacious
attempt to appeal over the head of the Janata government to
"industrial labour, farmers, the rural and urban poor, the minorities, the weaker sections and the middle classes"—that is, the
whole country. They saw the statement as a perfect example
of Nixonian rhetoric: she talked about "keeping away" from
"press publicity"as if she had a choice in the matter; she talked
about the end of thirty years of Congress rule as "the heavy
reverses . . . in the northern States;" she talked about accepting
"the full responsibility" but not the blame; she spoke of the
commissions as if they were investigating her period in office
instead of her abuse of that office.

Mrs. Gandhi followed her July statement with a pilgrimage,
in August, to the ashram of the ascetic Vinoba Bhave, in Paunar,
in central India. It was a bold step, calculated to draw wide
publicity. Bhave was the leading disciple of Mahatma Gandhi,
who was the patron saint of the Janata government, and for
years Bhave himself had been the patron saint of the Congress
governments—so much so that he was nicknamed Government
Saint. Bhave had first given his blessing to the Emergency, but
had later become wary of it, only to be harassed and lambasted
by the authorities. In June, 1976, Mrs. Gandhi's government
had actually raided his ashram as a warning to him against med-
dling in affairs of state. By her pilgrimage, she would be making
amends for the raid, and he, by receiving her, would be forgiving
her. Her pilgrimage caught the public imagination, and all along
the way she was greeted by throngs. She spent several days in
private consultations with the ascetic, sitting at his feet, talking
and meditating. She thus put the Janata leadership on notice
that she was not as helpless and powerless as they had thought.
And the pilgrimage seemed to have emboldened her. She made

it the start of a campaign for personal rehabilitation, and thereafter assumed an increasingly prominent public role. She came to feel so confident that in September she one day denied that Sanjay had had any responsibility for the excesses of the Emergency, and another day observed that she might well be Prime Minister again. In the new political climate, her friends began to explain away even her defeat in Rae Bareli, saying that her feckless staff took the campaign money, pocketed it, and sat on their hands, competing with one another to see who could get richer at her expense. It was no wonder, her friends said, that she rued the day she had ever trusted anyone. Her political emergence, coming, as it did, within six months of her staggering defeat, made some Janata leaders jittery about their own political prospects.

In private life, Mrs. Gandhi, with her sons, their wives, and her grandchildren, moved out of the official Prime Minister's residence in June into a big government bungalow allotted to them at a fair market price in a fashionable part of New Delhi, where she began working with a small staff of typists and assistants, most of whom were volunteers. She seldom accepted invitations to intimate gatherings, but one day in September she attended a small dinner, arriving in a chauffeur-driven Ambassador—an Indian-made car—with a government-provided bodyguard. At dinner, when she wasn't picking at her food she was nervously folding and unfolding a small handkerchief, cupping and twisting it in her hands. She kept blinking, as if she had something in her eye or had developed a twitch. She seemed bored and lonely and quite tense. Conversation was hesitant—discretion did not permit discussion of politics or any other controversial topic. She talked mostly about how difficult it was for her to find a good cook, how problematic it was to grow good avocados in India, and how children these days didn't get enough homework. Listening to her, one might have thought that she was a middle-class Indian housewife who had travelled abroad and tasted foreign avocados and who felt that servants and schools were not what they used to be. The occasion of the dinner was a sort of low-key celebration, for Mrs. Gandhi had just signed an agreement with her host, who was to write her official biography in order to prepare the way for her eventual "comeback."

For many months, Mrs. Gandhi's critics had been comparing her with Richard Nixon, pointing not only to the similarity of their rhetoric but to the contrast between their public and private faces, and referring to all the scandals connected with her regime as "India-gate." There actually is an India Gate in New Delhi; it is not an apartment complex but a war memorial.

3

Celibate
Janata Leaders

The Janata government had been in power only about six months when disillusion set in among members of the establishment. The old Indian arrogance, which often masked a deep sense of inferiority, was being tempered. Before the Emergency, Indian intellectuals had been ready with glib Marxist or Gandhian, even Stalinist or Hitlerian, solutions to Indian problems, but the taste of Emergency dictatorship and their disappointment in the professedly Gandhian Janata government had the effect of sobering them up.

The Ministers in Prime Minister Morarji Desai's Cabinet were the most parochial men to have ruled the country since Independence. They were more Indian in their background and outlook than Nehru and Mrs. Gandhi and many associates of theirs had been. They were preponderantly from the Hindi-speaking North, and few of them were particularly comfortable speaking English. Most of them were Hindus. Most of them had come to New Delhi by the route of local politics, through opposition or agitation. With the exception of H. M. Patel, the Janata Minister of Finance, none of them had distinguished themselves in the Indian civil or academic establishments, or attended an English or an American university, or studied at the Inns of

Court. None of them seemed to stand out above their colleagues, and none of them had a particular expertise. Most of them, in the normal course of events, could not have expected to wield national power, but they adapted to the trappings of it with remarkable agility, living and working, like their predecessors, out of sight of their constituents, who in India exist for the most part as shadows at the windows. They quickly mastered the art of keeping their names in the headlines and on the tip of people's tongues by generating teapot controversies in Parliament. Many of them shed their former political skins. The Janata Minister of Defense, Jagjivan Ram, who some months earlier had been ratifying Mrs. Gandhi's Emergency decisions, portrayed himself as her strongest opponent. (Since his defection had been one of the most important causes of Mrs. Gandhi's downfall, he was nicknamed J-Bomb.) The Janata Minister of External Affairs, Atal Bihari Vajpayee, who had been a rabble-rousing Hindi orator of the Hindu-chauvinist Jana Sangh Party, quickly became a secular rationalist. Perhaps the most gifted and most consistent of the Janata leaders, Chandra Shekhar, had been left out of the Cabinet. Instead, he had been given the thankless task of building up the Janata Party as its president.

The one Janata Minister who tenaciously clung to his old political skin was Raj Narain, the Minister of Health and Family Welfare, who was from the peasant-based Bharatiya Lok Dal wing of the Janata Party. In 1975, he had been the successful plaintiff in the Rae Bareli election case in which Mrs. Gandhi was the defendant, and in 1977 he had been the successful candidate in Rae Bareli, where Mrs. Gandhi lost to him by a wide margin. He took pride in having changed the course of Indian history single-handed and was nicknamed Giant-Killer, Bulldozer of Rae Bareli, and Stormy Petrol (the Indianism for "stormy petrel.") He bragged to a children's magazine that his devotion to the Hindu monkey-god, Hanuman, had given him strength to win the election. He became a folk hero and the subject of countless stories, some true, some apocryphal—though, given his eccentricities, it was not always easy to know which were which.

According to one story, he had sometimes campaigned in Rae Bareli sitting in a monkey's cage. He would stick his head out between the bars and say, "Take off your shoes and hit me on the head, hit me on my soul with the filthiest thing you have on you. I am responsible for the Emergency. I am responsible for all her crimes. If you elect her now, you will all be inside the cage, the whole country will be inside the cage."

Another story went that when he became Health Minister he summoned department bigwigs and asked them, "On whose authority did you sterilize your brothers?"

"Sir, you know who gave the order"

"Where is the order? Let me see it. Where is the paper with the order?"

"Sir, the order was never written down."

He gave each one of them a stone, made his clerk stand in the middle of the room, and said, "Stone this clerk! I order you!" He shouted, "I order you to throw a stone at him and you don't move, but when she ordered you, you didn't hesitate to take a knife to your brothers!"

In the early months of the Janata government, Raj Narain was in the papers every day with a new antic or a new controversy. His bizarre dress and conduct invited attention wherever he went. He always wore a green bandanna tied around his head and carried a shiny aluminum stick. In March, at the swearing-in ceremony of the new Cabinet, at Rashtrapati Bhavan, which is the residence of the President and so is one of the most august places in the country, he embarrassed everyone by bounding around and stuffing huge, sticky balls of sweetmeats into the mouths of Ministers as they were trying to look their sedate best on television.

As Janata Health Minister, Raj Narain became notorious

for his reception of visitors and officials. He received them in the Minister's bungalow with hardly a loincloth on him, while he was surrounded by dozens of cronies and was being massaged or shaved; during an interview he would crunch through a jar of roasted chickpeas without so much as making the gesture of offering any to his visitors. If someone spoke to him in English, he would point to his mouth and shake his head, like a rustic meeting an Englishman.

It is a Parliamentary courtesy that during the morning question period a Minister should answer a question in the language in which it was asked (provided he knows it). As many as fourteen languages are spoken in Parliament, and few subjects in India are as politically sensitive as the rights of linguistic minorities. In one question period, Raj Narain was asked a question in English; he started answering it in Hindi and created a furor. The members demanded that he start again and answer in English. But Raj Narain shouted in Hindi that he didn't know about their parents, but his mother and father and his grandparents all had only Indian blood. The remark was expunged from the record, but the slur became part of the public memory of the Janata government.

Raj Narain was born in 1917 into a landowning family near Benares, in what, in independent India, became Uttar Pradesh. Although at one time he weighed two hundred and forty-two pounds and cultivated a reputation for being the most powerful wrestler in Benares, practically his whole life was spent in politics. He was a political agitator as a student, and for nearly forty years he was active in the local politics of Uttar Pradesh, where he stretched Mahatma Gandhi's notion of civil disobedience and noncoöperation almost to its limits (he frequently led strikes, walked out of meetings, staged sitdowns, and disobeyed laws, all in the name of conscience), even as he became a follower of the socialist leader Dr. Ram Manohar Lohia, a firebrand of Indian politics who had made his reputation in part by being a

Nehru-baiter—thundering regularly against the Western, aristocratic attitudes of the Nehrus. In those years, Raj Narain belonged to one or another of the local socialist opposition parties, which were continually splintering and regrouping themselves. He became known for his riotous behavior in the Uttar Pradesh legislative assembly, and it has been estimated that between 1952 and 1962 he took up thirty per cent of its debating time with his antics. He was arrested at least fifty-eight times and spent a total of fifteen years in jail. Even in the councils of the socialists, Raj Narain always aroused controversy, and people said that Dr. Lohia came to regret having harbored him as a disciple. In fact, his old socialist party suspended him in 1971, just when he came into national prominence because of the Rae Bareli case.

As a member of the Janata government, he found himself in charge of a Ministry concerned with, among other things, the country's drinking water and sanitation—although in the political hierarchy of the Indian Cabinet the Health portfolio had a low priority and had traditionally been given to a weaker member. In the capital, he quickly developed a reputation as a jester and buffoon. In the Parliament, he indulged in disruptive antics, just as he had in the Uttar Pradesh legislative assembly, and outside the Parliament he dispensed with the proprieties of his position. Many of his "spoons" lived with him in the Minister's house; it was as if he were running a charity hostel in a village.

During the early days of his Janata Ministership, I cornered him one day in his office at Parliament House, and was astonished to discover that he was a prosaic fellow after all. He was in an ordinary kurta—a long, collarless, loose shirt—and pajamas, but was surrounded by his usual claque of talkative cronies, clerks, and hangers-on. When I told him that I would like to speak to him alone, he waved his aluminum stick at them, and they scurried like chickens into an anteroom, where they kept up a background hubbub.

I asked him whether some of the colorful stories about him
were true. He seemed drowsy and scarcely took in my question;
I rephrased it.

"What can I say?" he said, with a yawn. He picked his
teeth. "You should put your question to people who tell such
stories. I am a simple man. I only wear this green handkerchief
on my head as a green light, a signal to go ahead. It's the only
direction for the country and me to go."

"Did you actually campaign sitting in a monkey's cage?" I
asked.

"I don't remember, but let people say anything they like."

"Why have you gone to jail so often since Independence?"

"Because I felt that the Indian government was carrying
on traditions of British imperialism. I began my career of agitation as a student in the nineteen-thirties, when the British government increased our fees by fifty per cent. I opposed the raise
and went to jail. Since then, I have taken part in labor agitation,
peasant agitation, religious agitation, communal agitation, Untouchable agitation—every kind of agitation—and gone to jail
fifty-eight times."

"Were you ever afraid of going to jail?"

"Not at all. Outside the jail, I search for Brahma through
yoga, and inside the jail I search for Brahma through yoga."

"What happened to your family when you went to jail?"

"Nothing. I come from a joint-family system, and my wife
and children are the family's responsibility. I am the middle
brother of three brothers, and my elder brother takes care of
everything."

"Where are your wife and children now, and what are your
children doing?"

"I don't know. I have long been a *brahmachari* [celibate].
But I think my wife lives in Benares. I think one of my sons is
in agriculture or something like that, one is in government service
somewhere, and one is studying somewhere."

It was not always easy to make out what he was saying, because he kept worrying his teeth. Moreover, before answering each question he paused for a long time, as if mentally absenting himself from the room to consider the question. Sometimes I had to ask the question repeatedly before it seemed to register, and even then he would answer with a yawn. Sometimes he would obviously forget the question, and at one point he observed, "You notice I forget? It's because I am meditating."

"Do you believe in permanent agitation?"

"Agitation is for some time and revolution is for all time," he said wearily. "In revolution, there is a continuous flow—a flow of change."

I asked him about his lifelong feud with the Nehrus.

"I neither was nor am a foe of anyone," he said, picking his teeth. He went on to give a complicated history of his struggles with Nehru, with Nehru's sister, Mrs. Vijaya Lakshmi Pandit, with Mrs. Gandhi, with Sanjay—complete with dates and places, as if these marked battles in a Hindu epic.

I asked him how it felt finally to be a ruler after being a revolutionary for most of his life.

"Any work that God drafts me to do He has already given me the capacity to do," he said cryptically.

The main project that Raj Narain had put forward as Janata Health Minister was a scheme to have each village select a representative who would be given, at government expense, a three-month crash program in medicine, including nature cures—from Ayur-Vedic, Unani, and other ancient systems of medicine—and who would then return to his former occupation in his village but would function on the side as a sort of paraprofessional community-health worker. Raj Narain's critics contended that his scheme would not only misappropriate meagre resources but also debase medical standards and put legitimate and quack medicine on the same footing. I asked Raj Narain about his project.

"I'm not against allopathic medicine," he said. "I simply

want our ancient systems to enjoy equal status with it. As Health Minister, I am going to see to it that our systems are given due honor and respect."

"But are they equally valid scientifically?"

"I think they are," he said. "I have always treated myself with Ayur-Vedic medicine."

"But your Ministry has limited resources. If they are diverted to nature cures—Ayur-Vedic or whatever—then won't allopathic medicine suffer?"

"I think that the vote for Janata was a vote for our ancient tradition. I don't think standards of allopathic medicine will fall. Standards of our ancient systems will only rise."

Since he obviously didn't understand that allopathic medicine was scientific and nature cures were not, I turned to the problem of population. There is no problem in India more serious than that. Sanjay's forced-sterilization program during the Emergency had aroused such strong opposition that, people said, it had set back by years what little headway the country had made in controlling population growth. So far, the Janata government had done nothing about the problem. It had even changed the formal name of Raj Narain's Ministry from Health and Family Planning to Health and Family Welfare—this at a time when sociologists were suggesting that the whole population problem had been mishandled by the government since Independence and required rethinking. Government attention from the beginning, they said, had been directed almost entirely toward changing personal preference in order to limit families, though in the Indian context caste, class, and community pressures might have had more to do with family size. I asked Raj Narain about family planning.

"I am completely against compulsion," he said. "I think we should try the old method of self-control and sexual abstinence. If you properly educate our people, they will follow our old method. After all, God Rama had only two children."

66

Two and a half months after Morarji Desai succeeded Mrs. Gandhi as Prime Minister, and she vacated the official residence, he moved in, with his family: his wife, Gajraben; his younger sister, a childless widow; and his son, Kantilal. (The Desais have only one other child living—a daughter, who is married and lives in Bombay.)

The Desais were known to be a family of fixed habits, who had always lived parsimoniously. Even when Desai was in jail, every household expense was cleared with him. Their sole indulgence used to be that they kept a pair of cows for fresh milk. The only major change they made in the Prime Minister's residence was to rip out one of Mrs. Gandhi's bathrooms and install an old-fashioned Indian-style bathroom—with no such modern conveniences as a bathtub—for Mrs. Desai, who preferred to bathe with a bucket and a dipper. Desai moved into the two rooms that had served as Mrs. Gandhi's study and bedroom, but he made Mrs. Gandhi's study into his bedroom and Mrs. Gandhi's bedroom into his study. He slept alone in his bedroom—its walls were bare except for a painting of Swami Ramakrishna Paramahamsa, one of Desai's gurus—on a hard bed with *khadi,* or homespun, sheets and pillowcases. He would wake at four o'clock in the morning and for three hours say his prayers, do his yoga exercises, and make his ablutions. He would open his door shortly before seven and take in the newspapers but would look only at the headlines, because he felt that he didn't have time to read the stories. From seven to ten, he would either receive visitors by appointment in the living room or see the crowds of people who had gathered outside his residence. Some simply wanted his darshana, and they were quickly disposed of. Others had grievances, and whenever he could, he lent an ear to their petitions and told them whom to see or what to do. At ten o'clock, he would go into his dining room and have his first meal of the day, while the members of his family—who had already eaten—sat and watched him. In the past, he had eaten a vegetarian diet cooked in pure ghi, but after his time in jail during the Emergency he had given up vegetables and cereals. Now he avoided "sour fruits," because they gave him gas, and would eat only "sweet fruits"—mangoes, litchis, bananas, apples, pears, cherries, apricots, papayas, in season. He would also drink fresh milk—a litre a day. It was served to him lukewarm, with plenty of cream on top, and with a special root powder dissolved in it to settle his stomach; like sour fruit, milk without the powder gave him gas. He would also regularly drink a glass of his own morning urine, claiming that the practice, which he had kept up for much of his adult life, was responsible for his robust health—and he frequently and publicly recommended it to one and all. (He avoided modern medicine and relied on nature cures. He had never taken an injection, and in 1958 a special exception had to be made for him to permit him to enter the United States without a smallpox vaccination. "My opposition to inoculation and vaccination is on conscientious grounds," he has written. "I would not like my survival or well-being to be purchased at the expense of the suffering or loss of life of another living creature. You know the cruelty involved in the extraction of vaccines from animals. I shun vaccination or inoculation, therefore, just as much as I shun non-vegetarian food.") At eleven o'clock, Desai would go to Parliament if it was in session, or to the Prime Minister's office, either in Parliament House or in the Secretariat, where he would remain until about six-thirty, doing paperwork, seeing officials and colleagues, giving interviews, holding Cabinet meetings in a nearby room. He would have a second meal around seven, this time also eating handfuls of cashews, almonds, and dried fruit—dates were his favorite. At nine-thirty, he would go into his rooms and close the door.

Desai's day and diet did allow some variations, however. When he visited London in 1977 for the Commonwealth Prime

Ministers' Conference, his staff sent out this circular to, among other places, Buckingham Palace, which was planning some entertainment for the Commonwealth Prime Ministers:

Breakfast—8 A.M. A glass of boiled water (without ice) at room temperature. Carrot juice—only when deep pink carrots grown in Northern India are available in winter season. Narial Pani [coconut milk], when carrots are not in season. . . .

Lunch—1 P.M. Raw garlic (five pieces) Gujarat type; generally there are two cloves in one piece. These should be peeled and washed properly before serving. Half a litre of cow's milk (lukewarm) with no sugar. Honey (two small creamer full) to be served separately. Or half a litre curd prepared from cow's milk. It should not be sour at all. Fresh panir [cheese] slices—plain (no salt, pepper, etc.) prepared from cow's milk: 50 gms. . . . Dry fruits—cashewnuts (50 gms), badam [almonds] (20 gms), pista [pistachios] (10 gms) and moongphali dana [peanuts], roasted (50 gms). Indian sweets prepared from cow's milk. . . .

At 1530 hours the Prime Minister takes fresh apple juice (not sour) or tender coconut water/watermelon juice (without ice).

Dinner—7 P.M. Raw garlic—(five pieces) Gujarat type. . . . Half a litre of cow's milk (lukewarm). Fresh seasonal fruits (not sour). Dry fruits—dates (100 gms) figs (100 gms) cashewnuts (50 gms); moongphali dana roasted (50 gms) badam (20 gms) and pista (10 gms). . . .

In 1966, Desai had published a collection of articles and speeches entitled "In My View." A characteristic passage goes:

Once I had discussions with two friends who started accusing me of obstancy and rigidity. I asked them why they did so. At first they claimed that I had not heard their case. I countered with the question whether I had not listened to them patiently and argued with them for over an hour. To this their rejoinder was that while I had heard them, I had failed to accept their view.

Thus, they had confessed that the first charge was inadmissible. Then was it right to brand me as obstinate just because I had remained unconvinced that their point of view was acceptable? On the contrary, it might be that they themselves were obstinate in that they were not prepared to withdraw their accusation against me. This is how a false reputation is sought to be foisted upon me.

Trying to redeem that "false reputation" by turning the tables on his critics has preoccupied Desai for much of his long political career, his most sustained effort being a three-volume autobiography, "The Story of My Life." In the preface, Desai tells us that he felt he had to write the book, because "it was my duty to write about my experiences so that the reader might get some guidance from them when he is confused." This prefatory remark sets the didactic tone of the book, in which "God" and "proper," along with "I," appear with benumbing regularity. A little like Dr. Pangloss, Desai believes that everything that happens in the world is ultimately for the best, because it is God's will. It seems that the "I" is always right and is doing what is "proper":

> Till 1929 I used to scold my children and even punish them physically if they lied or did some mischief causing destruction of something. I had been considering the necessity of controlling my anger from 1921, but as I considered it also necessary to use it for getting work done, I did not succeed in my efforts to control it. I realized in 1929 that I should not try to improve my children or others by physical punishment. They were born with the influences of their past lives and I could not make any improvement in them by punishing them harshly and it was also not proper for me to do so. Moreover, they were not able to retaliate when

I punished them. It was, therefore, not proper for me to punish them physically. I, therefore, gave up giving physical punishment to my children from 1929.

Morarji, a Brahman and one of six children, was born on the intercalary day of February 29, 1896, in Gujarat. His father was a schoolteacher and headmaster of a village school. When the boy was fifteen, his father committed suicide by jumping into a well just three days before Morarji's arranged marriage to the eleven-year-old Gajraben. Morarji went through with the marriage on the appointed day and became the head of the family, which included—in addition to his child bride—his grandmother, his mother, three brothers, and two sisters. Soon after his wedding, however, he won a scholarship to Wilson College, in Bombay, and there he studied physics and developed a lifelong interest in watching cricket. He graduated in 1917, was granted a fellowship at his college for a year, and then joined Bombay's provincial civil service, in which he spent the next twelve years, mostly working as a revenue officer and magistrate.

In 1930, Desai left the British service to follow Mahatma Gandhi. Even before that, he had begun wearing *khadi,* had taken the vow of *brahmacharya,* after fathering three sons and two daughters, and had started experimenting with different kinds of simple diets. He became a member of the local Gujarat Congress committee, went to jail for anti-British activities, and came to the notice of the president of the committee, Sardar Vallabhbhai Patel. In 1937, when Congress provincial governments were formed under the British scheme of limited autonomy for India, Desai was elected to the provincial assembly from his home district and became revenue minister in Bombay's government, which was led by Chief Minister B. B. G. Kher. In 1939, all the Congress ministries resigned to protest the British commitment of India to war without the country's consent, and Congress leaders and workers began a protracted political strug-

A Family Affair

gle against the British. Along with many others, Desai spent much of the time during the war in jail. In 1946, Kher formed a new government in Bombay, and for the next six years Desai served as its home minister, earning a reputation as a puritan zealot: he decreed that all students must use old-fashioned penholders with nibs and that all restaurants must close by midnight; he banned kissing in films; he campaigned against cosmetics and brothels; above all, he introduced total prohibition, which, like many of his other measures, was ultimately unsuccessful. In 1952, in part because of his moral crusades, he was not reëlected. But Kher soon retired and made Desai his successor, and after that Desai did manage to get himself reëlected.

As chief minister of Bombay, Desai is remembered mainly for ruthlessly putting down the agitation for division of the province on linguistic lines, between the Gujaratis and the Maharashtrians. He took the view that, in principle, Indians were one people, and should no more be divided by their languages than by their religions, say, and he reportedly ordered the police to shoot agitators at sight. Many of the agitators were students and workers, and Desai became, in the words of the *Illustrated Weekly,* "the most hated person" in the province. He even had trouble addressing public meetings in his own constituency. Although his moral edicts and police measures earned the undying enmity of the ruling middle class, he acquired a reputation for being a man of high principle, and, with it, a national following among Gandhians and the poor. (In 1960, two linguistically separate states—Maharashtra and Gujarat—came into being.)

In 1956, Desai moved to New Delhi, where, in Nehru's government, he served as Minister for Commerce and Industries until 1958, and then, from 1958 to 1963, as Minister of Finance. (In 1958, when he was sixty-two years old, he went out of the country for the first time, travelling in Europe, the United States, and Canada.) As Finance Minister, he is best remembered for promulgating the Gold Control Order, which prohibited the production of any gold jewelry purer than fourteen carats. He thereby antagonized more people than ever, because of the prominent place that gold jewelry has always had in the dowry of an Indian woman. In 1963, he was forced out of the Nehru Cabinet under the Kamaraj Plan—named after Kamaraj, the chief minister of the southern state of Madras, who, after some reverses in the previous year's general elections and some defeats in by-elections in the spring of 1963, had called on Congress leaders to resign from high office and work for the Party.

Upon Nehru's death, in 1964, Desai tried to buck Kamaraj (who had been made the Congress Party president in the interval) and become Prime Minister, but Kamaraj outmaneuvered him by putting forward Lal Bahadur Shastri as a consensus Congress candidate. Shastri won easily. In 1965, there was again bitter agitation over language, this time on a national scale. People in the South, who had grown up with English as their lingua franca, wanted to retain English in the courts, Parliament, and the civil service; people in the North, who used Hindi as their lingua franca, wanted to make Hindi the official national language. Desai became a leader of the Hindi movement, alienating people in the southern half of the country. When Shastri died suddenly, in 1966, Desai wasted no time in making a second bid for the Prime Ministership. He was probably the most prominent Congress leader, Kamaraj notwithstanding, but he had alienated students and workers, who looked upon him as a sort of Genghis Khan in *khadi;* Westernized Indians, who derided his moral crusade as a frustrated *brahmachari's* vengeance against the modern world; members of the Congress Party under Kamaraj's thumb, who thought of him as a Party Judas; women, who felt that his Gold Control Order was an attack on their life security; and many politicians, north and south. Chief ministers—the Party bosses—representing most of the important states got together and put forward Mrs. Gandhi as their candidate. Desai had had his suspicions all along that Nehru wanted his daughter to somehow become Prime Minister, and that the Kamaraj Plan and the consensus candidacy of Shastri were part of a larger scheme to realize Nehru's wishes—or why would a mere "schoolgirl," as Desai liked to call Mrs. Gandhi, be seriously put forward to run the country? He felt confident that the rank and file would see through the ignoble dynastic scheme and vote for him, but he overestimated his own popularity and underestimated the power of Kamaraj and the magic of the Nehru name. Mrs. Gandhi defeated him two to one.

Desai originally refused to join Mrs. Gandhi's Cabinet, but after the Congress suffered reverses in the elections of 1967 he was prevailed upon to become the Deputy Prime Minister and was given the Finance portfolio. His performance both in Parliament and in councils of the Party was so skillful and the force of his will and personality so evident that he almost came to exert decisive influence in the making of policy. He cast himself in the role of conciliator between the conservative wing of the Party, with which he had been identified, and the socialist wing, with which Mrs. Gandhi was identified. But Mrs. Gandhi didn't like being upstaged, and she found an opportunity to undermine his position. In 1969, there was an angry debate in the Party about nationalization of the banks. The conservatives wanted the banks to remain in private hands; Mrs. Gandhi and the socialists wanted the government to nationalize them. Desai, though conservative, tried to steer a middle course, and advocated something called "social control." The socialists and Mrs. Gandhi had all the votes, and they resoundingly routed the conservatives and Desai. In the meantime, the Party, with Mrs. Gandhi's support, had put up the conservative Neelan Sanjiva Reddy for President of India, but at the last minute Mrs. Gandhi, nerved by her success, put forward an elderly former trade unionist, V. V. Giri, as an anti-conservative, anti-boss candidate, in the name of socialism and democracy. Giri won. As a result of the bank and election controversies, Mrs. Gandhi and the socialists captured the organization of the Party, and the conservatives, with Desai as their chairman, were shunted aside as another Congress splinter group and became the Old Congress. Desai's long political career had seemingly come to an inglorious end (much as Mrs. Gandhi's seemingly had eight years later, after her March defeat), and his return to power appeared improbable.

From 1969 to the advent of the Emergency, Desai sat with the insignificant opposition in Parliament, as leader of the Old Congress. In April, 1975, he undertook a Mahatma Gandhi-style fast—his fifth—to force Mrs. Gandhi to hold elections in Gujarat. He succeeded, and the elections, which went against the Congress, became one of the immediate causes of the Emergency. The Emergency transformed what many had considered to be Desai's faults of character—obstinacy and rigidity—into virtues when, as a political prisoner of Mrs. Gandhi, he pitted his will against hers.

Over the years, one of Desai's main hobbies had been baiting the press, and time had not diminished his enthusiasm for the sport, as part of an account of a press conference in the Indian weekly the *Current,* published in the first, heady months of Janata rule, makes evident:

> "It's a waste of time," quipped one correspondent at the end of [Desai's] last press conference, "his and ours." . . . He is the prime specimen of evasive repartee. . . .
> Q: "When could we expect the full cabinet?"
> A: "Why are you so eager about it? None of you is a candidate."
> Q: "Your budget has been disappointing for the common man?"
> A: "If there is no disappointment for you, there will be no disappointment for the people. . . ."
> As a parting shot, a pressman refers to Morarjibhai's [Brother Morarji's] confessional statement that he changed

a lot after his [Emergency] jail term. "What is the nature of the change?" he asks, with a touch of irony.

"The change," says the Prime Minister, "is that now I know you better."

It was, however, not easy to know *him* better. I had first met Desai in 1959, when, as Finance Minister, he was one of Nehru's main lieutenants; at that meeting he had been full of himself and had scarcely concealed his eagerness to sit in Nehru's chair. Presiding over his office in the Secretariat, he had talked about the great future he envisioned for India. I had last met him in 1974, when he was a political nonentity and was helping to run various Gandhi trusts, committees, and museums—all busy guarding, perpetuating, and overseeing the memory of his mentor, who was venerated but unheeded in the country, much as Desai himself was, in a minor way, at the time. During that meeting, he had inveighed against Mrs. Gandhi as a latter-day Hindu Jezebel as he sat magisterially in the living room of his house—a large pink building—surrounded by a clutter of gods, saints, and curios: the Buddha; the Hindu elephant-god, Ganesh; pictures of Mahatma Gandhi; statues of the three "no-evil" monkeys; a silver replica of a cathedral; a pink plastic replica of a temple with pictures of Krishna pasted on the sides. In 1977, a few months after he became Prime Minister, I called on him in Parliament House, where he sat solemnly at one end of a boomerang-shaped table in Mrs. Gandhi's old office. Its furnishings included leather chairs, a sofa, a couple of paintings—one showing a woman on a horse. Except for adding a pen-and-ink drawing of Mahatma Gandhi, Desai had left the office exactly as it was.

Desai got up slowly, and vigorously shook my hand—a tall and handsome man, with strong, cruel features, like those of a bird of prey. He was wearing glasses with heavy brown plastic frames, a starched Gandhi cap, a Nehru jacket, a white kurta, and tight pajamas bunched up around his calves.

I asked him what it felt like to be sitting in Mrs. Gandhi's chair.

"I am doing God's will," he said sternly.

"What does it mean to you to be doing God's will?"

"Understanding that requires faith," he said. "And since you have no faith in God, I can't convince you about what I mean."

"It is not a matter of convincing me but of describing what doing God's will means to you."

"Do you believe in God?" he asked me belligerently.

"You seem to be parrying my question."

"No, I am not parrying," he said scoldingly. "If you have faith in God, you believe that you are His instrument, and that God acts in the world through His law, and that His law is responsible for the whole universe. Everything in the universe happens according to that law. You have only to fit in with the law."

I wanted to bring the conversation back to the here and now, but in order to enter into the spirit of his talk I asked him if Mrs. Gandhi had fallen from office because she hadn't fitted in with the law.

"Not quite," he said, getting interested. "It means that people like her don't *try* to fit in with the law. They try to fit in with themselves; they're all egoists."

I saw that there was no easy way to change the direction of the talk, and so I asked him, "Is not everyone, in a sense, an egoist?"

"I'm not an egoist," he replied, with a disarming lack of self-awareness. "I have eliminated my ego altogether."

"Do you really imagine that you can eliminate your ego?"

"That is what I mean when I say to myself, 'What am I

doing here in the Prime Minister's office? I am doing nothing—
I am only doing God's law.' "

I asked him to tell me in concrete terms how he planned
to put that law into practice as Prime Minister.

"If I had perfectly perceived God's law, I would not be
sitting here. I want to perceive God through the service of men,
because this is all His creation. If you go to some people's homes
and please their children, the parents feel very happy. That happi-
ness can snowball—I think if I can please all the children I will
be nearer Him, I will be nearer God."

He came across as a man who took everything literally, and
who seemed impervious to the person he was speaking to.

I asked him how his health was standing up under the pressures of his office.

"There's nothing wrong with my health. It's as good as an
old man's health can be." He blew his nose, and said that because
of the changeable weather his nose had been running and that
he had been treating himself with some nature cures, like washing
his nose out with salt water and eating garlic.

I asked him about his eccentric diet.

"There's nothing strange about it. It happens to be made
up of the healthiest food there is. I think it's the healthiest food
for everybody to eat, but everybody's not convinced that I'm
right. You see, everybody has his likes and dislikes. But, ultimately, it comes down to this—that taste is more a matter of
the mind than of the tongue. If it were a matter of the tongue,
then everybody would like the same thing, since the tongue is
constructed of the same material in everybody. So likes and dislikes are therefore only a matter of self-control—abstinence. If
you take tea for several days, you get into the habit of taking
tea, and then you like tea. Therefore, it is most important to
control your mind before you take the tea. Before you can control
your mind, you must control your sexual urges. If you don't
control your sexual urges, you won't have the energy to control

your mind properly. Sexual impulses are the main disturbing impulses in life."

Desai was only engaging in the traditional Gandhian rhetoric of celibacy, taking refuge in an all too Hindu kind of deductive reasoning. I didn't pursue the subject. Instead, I said, "People say that your last term in jail has mellowed you, and that you've become more charitable toward other people's failings. Would you say that you have changed?"

"I am changing every day. Every person ought to change every day if he wants to be better than he was the day before. You should also try to change every day. I'm happy that you recognize that I have changed. But it is not a question of my being charitable toward other people's failings. The change people speak of is my ability to appreciate other people's points of view better than I could before."

"How does it feel to be Prime Minister finally? You have wanted the office for many years."

"Here, again, people have got some wrong notions about me. I've never wanted anything for myself."

"Now that you're Prime Minister, what do you most hope to accomplish?"

"To serve India in the best way I can."

"Do you think your wish to serve may be frustrated by the bureaucracy, for example?"

"I will never be frustrated. Why should I be frustrated? A man with real faith in God can never be frustrated."

"Before the Emergency, you were considered to be the most authoritarian person in Indian politics."

"People say anything they like. I'm just firm when I know I'm right."

I observed that he was a good debater.

"If you debate with me, should I not debate with you?"

I said politely that I would lose my debate with him.

"If you lose the debate, is it my fault? I hear you patiently.

If you ask me to argue, I will argue. If you ask me to hear only, I will hear you. If you argue with me, I will argue with you. If I don't argue with you, you will say I am not arguing with you. If I argue with you, and if you don't find a counterargument sufficient to demolish my argument, will that be my fault? Would that be authoritarian? Is that why I'm thought to be authoritarian?"

I had been swept along by the pyrotechnics of his conversation, but now I stood my ground and pressed home several of the questions on my mind.

"Do you and the Janata Party have a radical social and economic program for the country?"

"Unlike the previous government, we think planning should be for people, not people for planning. Therefore, our planning will satisfy people's needs and people's aspirations."

"It is said that you took agitators like Raj Narain and George Fernandes into your Cabinet not because they were the most talented men available but because you felt they would be more dangerous outside the Cabinet than they would be in it."

"Who is the right kind of man to be a Minister? Will you define it for me? Ideally, no one is fit to be a Minister. But you should remember, if people have spent all their lives in opposition they cannot immediately get accustomed to exercising power. But giving them power teaches them how to use it."

I tried to steer him to the subject of the endless finger-pointing, recriminations, and inquiries that the government was carrying on. (Desai's apologists said that he would have liked to set a lofty tone for the government, but that those of his colleagues who, like Charan Singh, had powerful constituencies of their own would not permit him to be master in his own house.) I observed, "Your government seems to be preoccupied more with Mrs. Gandhi and the Emergency than with the problems of the country, and it is now being said that Charan Singh is so vindictive that he won't rest until he has brought Sanjay and Mrs. Gandhi to trial and put them in jail."

"I don't know about Charan Singh—ask him. Is it right that I should give opinions on my colleagues? If I give good opinions about my colleagues, you will say I am doing so because they are my colleagues. If I don't give good opinions about my colleagues, you will say that I am not standing by them."

"Is your Janata government different from former—Congress—governments in substance or only in style?"

"That's for people to decide. We shall say that we are different in substance."

"How would you characterize the difference?"

"In every way. In the first place, we believe in democracy without any strings. The last government didn't believe in it. That's why they failed. In the second place, we believe in Gandhiji's methods and values and we hope to bring society around to them."

"How, exactly, will you go about following Mahatma Gandhi's methods?"

"What Gandhiji said was that before you do anything you should put before your mind the needs of the poorest man in the country and see if what you are going to do is going to help him or not help him. Therefore, we plan to concentrate on rural India and make the life of the poorest man richer— not in money but in every other way."

"The sentiment is unexceptionable, but how do you plan to put it into practice? Will you allocate more money in the budget for rural development?"

"We will allocate more money if it's necessary. But what is required first is that everyone should have employment, and no one should be unemployed. This will have to be done by the government and various volunteer agencies. The government role will be mostly in convincing the villager that there is something *he* can do for himself and then seeing to it that he does this with brilliance and enthusiasm, and then the volunteer agency will give him that something to do."

Tens of millions of people are unemployed in India, and his goal seemed visionary, but it was difficult to get him to admit that. Mahatma Gandhi used to say that he was the only Gandhian, but after his death Gandhism had been made into something of an orthodoxy, the Gandhian aficionados forming a sort of clique, who were constantly in touch with one another but out of touch with the modern world. They reduced the ideas and ideals of Gandhi to rigid strictures on diet, dress, and nature cures. So I asked Desai whether Gandhians had anything to do with the spirit of Gandhi.

"The followers of all prophets are rigid," he said offhandedly. "Rigidity is its own form of truth. The expert is the one who is the most dogmatic, and Gandhiji needs expert interpreters."

"The Janata Party is made up of such disparate elements—do you think they will all be able to work together?"

"They have now all accepted the Gandhian philosophy."

"But Indian politicians have always paid lip service to Gandhian philosophy."

"We don't propose to do that."

"Will you, then, cut some of the defense expenditure?"

"Cutting defense doesn't mean Gandhism."

I had to remind myself that Desai had won his colors in Indian politics, which, even as the treacherous domain of politics goes, is notorious for being coarse and rough. For him to have survived in it at all was to have distinguished himself as an armadillo among men. I therefore tried to turn the conversation to his hopes and aspirations. "As you look ahead to the next five or ten years, do you think you will be able to do things Mrs. Gandhi was unable to do?"

"In ten years, India will be the happiest country in the world."

"You really believe that?"

"Yes, I do. This is my intense belief."

"How can you hope to make even an impression on Indian poverty?"

"Why not?" he asked impatiently, and he added, as an after-thought, "I don't want to be first in the world in gross national product, first in the world in per-capita income. I don't want the affluence of the West for India. Like Gandhiji, I only want a good life for every Indian."

"And you really think that this is possible in the next ten or whatever number of years?"

"It's certainly possible in the next ten years, or why would I be sitting here? We have in India the resources, the intelligence, the capacity for hard work, and, above all, we have faith. I may see God in this life or in the next life or in several lives. It's all in the hands of God."

4

Family
Squabbles

On April 29, 1978, Charan Singh resigned from the National Executive and Central Parliamentary Board of the Janata Party, largely in protest against Desai's failure to act in the matter of Kantilal. Disenchantment with Desai's rule was growing in the Party and in the country, and both Jaya Prakash Narayan and J. B. Kripalani openly regretted having selected him as Prime Minister.

Just then, the Shah Commission completed its report, which was based on seven months of public hearings, and forwarded it to the Cabinet. The report catalogued and described innumerable instances of the Emergency government's violations of human rights and abuses of power, of corruption on the part of Mrs. Gandhi and Sanjay, and of subversion by them of the constitution, the judiciary, the civil service, and the military during the Emergency. The indictment of the Emergency and of the mother and son was so sweeping that it surprised even some of Mrs. Gandhi's critics. The Cabinet, still split between hawks and doves, made no move except to appoint a committee to process the report and its recommendations for preventing future corruption and subversion of the government and the constitution.

Charan Singh, who was still the Home Minister, seemed

incensed that, even armed with the evidence of the Shah Commission, the government refused to act. He had been growing increasingly restive at not having his hawkish way. He was getting nowhere with several new minor cases he had been forced to institute against Mrs. Gandhi (one of them concerned her wrongful "detention" of some textile inspectors), and he felt that the court proceedings, as in the earlier cases, had the effect of caricaturing the enormity of her crimes. He often complained that her supporters rioted outside the courtroom whenever she or Sanjay appeared in court; that her lawyers skillfully parried the prosecutors and won delay after delay; that she and her associates ridiculed the commissions of inquiry as mere partisan bodies engaged in a witch-hunt. He drew attention to the fact that Mrs. Gandhi, emboldened by the Janata government's self-advertised impotence, was travelling all over the country deriding the government and stirring up discontent; everywhere, he said, she was haranguing street crowds with inflammatory speeches, inciting them to riot, and so obliging the police to disperse them forcibly, and then asking the next street crowd she addressed what sort of government it was that could not even insure law and order.

Charan Singh devised a plan for establishing special courts for the speedy trial of people who had held high public office, so that Mrs. Gandhi, Sanjay, and their associates could be quickly tried for their Emergency crimes, and he got an opinion from the highest legal authorities in the country that such special courts would be within the framework of the constitution and could be established merely by the promulgation of an ordinance. But he did not take his proposal immediately to the Cabinet, ostensibly because Desai was failing him at every turn. There was, for instance, the matter of H. N. Bahuguna and his son Vijay. Bahuguna, a Brahman member of the Congress for Democracy, was the Minister of Petroleum, Chemicals, and Fertilizers, and had been Charan Singh's main rival when both of them were in regional politics in Uttar Pradesh. They had both served as chief minister of Uttar Pradesh, and had vied with one another for the control of its affairs. A deep animosity had grown up between them. On April 2nd, Charan Singh had written to Desai reminding him that he was supposed to be looking into many charges of corruption levelled against Bahuguna ("I will refer here only to some of them. According to a report submitted to the former P.M. on 25.11.1975, Shri Bahuguna had received substantial financial advantage in cases relating to the disposal of the power station at Harduaganj [in Aligarh] to the Modis. . . . The Modis were principal financiers of Shri Bahuguna and they were shown undue favours in the form of lesser octroi duty, purchase of shares and appointment of Shri K. N. Modi as Chairman of the Provincial Investment Industrial Corporation. . . . These charges came to your notice formally four months ago, but to no avail"); that Bahuguna's son was also corrupt ("His son, Vijay Bahuguna, a young advocate, aged twenty-eight years, was appointed a retainer by several big companies"); that Bahuguna was probably a traitor ("Shri Bahuguna is in close touch with the Communist Party of India and is its great supporter. Through it he has tried to establish contacts with the U.S.S.R. In fact, he is regarded in some circles as an agent of the K.G.B. In 1974 and 1975 the U.S.S.R. is reported to have thought of grooming him as a possible successor to Smt. [Mrs.] Indira Gandhi"); that Bahuguna had unfairly attacked the writer of the letter ("Immediately after the Janata Government had taken over at the Centre, I am told, Shri Bahuguna got two scurrilous pamphlets published in Lucknow, painting me in the darkest possible colours—one of which I had brought to your notice as long ago as in March 1977. . . . You [could] restrain Shri Bahuguna who is a member of your Cabinet if only you would, but you have not"); and that Desai, having been apprised of many of these facts, continued to keep Bahuguna in the Cabinet ("On January 15, 1978, Shri Shibban Lal Saxena, a Member of Parliament . . . wrote to you a longer letter detailing a hundred and one instances of Shri H. N. Bahuguna's misconduct or corruption: 'I am amazed that a man of this character who is an incarnation of Satan himself . . . should be a member of the Cabinet of the Government of India. . . . I have therefore thought it my duty to bring the aforesaid facts to your notice for a thorough inquiry by the C.B.I. [Central Bureau of Investigation]. Meanwhile if you think I have made a prima facie case against Shri H. N. Bahuguna, you should immediately remove him from your Central Cabinet. I hope you will pardon me for the trouble I am giving you. But I thought it my duty to undertake this labour of love for the last four months. Such a man should be exposed mercilessly and given just and deterrent punishment, so that no other person may dare to follow in the steps of this Shri NATWAR LAL [Mr. Scoundrel]!' ").

On June 28th, Charan Singh, for whatever reason, made public his plan for the special courts—a plan he had still not discussed with his Cabinet colleagues—and his criticism of Desai and the Cabinet for not taking action against Mrs. Gandhi. From his bed at the Suraj Kund, a resort a few miles from Delhi, where he was convalescing from a heart attack, he gave an interview to the press in which he said, among other things, "Perhaps those [in the Cabinet] who differ from me do not realize sufficiently the intensity of the feelings among the people of our country on the government's failure to put the former Prime Minister behind bars by now. They draw all sorts of conclusions and are inclined to give credence to all kinds of stories. They think that we in the government are a pack of impotent people who cannot govern the country. . . . It only represents their patriotic reaction to the manner in which Mrs. Gandhi and her caucus have tried to denigrate the law courts, create uproars in law-court compounds, impute motives to the Shah Commission, subvert the prosecution evidence, and generally create an atmosphere of violence and terror in the country against those who differed from her and Congress." (As it happened, one of the reasons that Mrs. Gandhi had given for the proclamation of the Emergency was that her opponents were doing what she was now accused of doing: creating conditions that made the maintenance of law and order impossible—conditions that, according to her, had made it necessary for her to put these opponents behind bars.)

Desai immediately wrote to Charan Singh asking for his resignation, on the ground that by going to the press over the heads of his colleagues he had violated the principle of "the Cabinet's collective responsibility." At the same time, he dismissed Charan Singh's closest Bharatiya Lok Dal ally, Raj Narain, saying that by his criticisms outside the Parliament he, too, had brought the Janata government "into disrepute in the public eye."

Charan Singh resigned on June 30th, but charged on the floor of the Parliament that Desai's letter to him was couched in "the language of a master to a servant," and that although Desai scolded him now for supposedly transgressing the principle of "the Cabinet's collective responsibility," Desai never honored it himself, for he never spoke in terms of "we" or "the Cabinet" or "the government" but always in terms of "I." In any case, Charan Singh said, if Desai had a real reason for complaint, why hadn't he bothered to talk to him first instead of summarily dismissing him? "Admitting I tarried or failed in my duty of sending up proposals in regard to Mrs. Gandhi's trial [by special courts] promptly to the Cabinet," he said, "could not the Prime Minister motor down to the Suraj Kund for a discussion with me, or, if he considered this course to be below his dignity, could he not ring me up for a telephonic talk?" (Charan Singh's statement, like many exchanges quoted in these pages, was written in what is called Indian English.)

Desai may have thought that Charan Singh, Raj Narain, and their friends (four junior Ministers from the Bharatiya Lok

89

Dal resigned in sympathy) were more disruptive inside the Cabinet than out of it and that he could govern perfectly well without them. But the president of the Janata Party, Chandra Shekhar, and the leaders of the Socialists and the Jana Sangh thought otherwise, and they set about trying to mediate the quarrel. They feared that Charan Singh might cause a further split in the Janata ranks and thereby jeopardize the effectiveness of the Janata government. Charan Singh had called a demonstration of his supporters for July 17th, which threatened to become a replay of the December birthday rally and encourage further defections. The mediators had Charan Singh call off the demonstration, and they arranged at least three meetings between him and Desai.

Charan Singh subsequently claimed that at each of these meetings Desai had pressed him to withdraw his demand for a commission of inquiry concerning Kantilal's conduct as a precondition for his return to the Cabinet, and that each time he had refused. He claimed that during his meetings with Desai he had come to the conclusion that he had been forced to resign merely because of his agitation for such a commission of inquiry, and that the principle of "the Cabinet's collective responsibility" had been only Desai's "pretext" for a coverup. On the floor of the Parliament, Charan Singh, recapitulating the history of his relationship with Desai, remarked, "In his abounding affection for his son, Shri Desai does not realize that he has done great harm to the Janata Party, the public life of the country, and to democracy."

The Official Congress Party had continued to enjoy a majority in the Council of States, or upper house of Parliament—its members were mostly elected by state legislative assemblies under a system of staggered biennial elections, in contrast to the House of the People, or lower house, whose members were elected by the people every five years or, of course, whenever Parliament was dissolved—and the Official Congress leaders saw in the affair of Charan Singh and Desai an opportunity to embarrass the government. In August, the upper house passed a resolution demanding that the charges of corruption against the family members of both Charan Singh and Desai be investigated. Although Desai insisted that without the concurring vote of the lower house the resolution was not binding, it did put additional pressure on him. Desai, who had refrained from filling the Ministerial chairs of Charan Singh and Raj Narain, now offered to take Charan Singh back if he simply apologized for his insinuations about Kantilal. Charan Singh said that he would come back only if he was made Deputy Prime Minister. The designation of Deputy Prime Minister was honorific and was seldom actually used, but for all practical purposes it belonged to Jagjivan Ram, who had a national following, in contrast to Charan Singh's regional one. Even though Charan Singh's Bharatiya Lok Dal had a much larger representation in the Parliament than Jagjivan Ram's Congress for Democracy, everyone thought that Jagjivan Ram, who was among the vainest men in politics, would sooner leave the Cabinet than take second place to Charan Singh. Then, in November, Mrs. Gandhi made what looked like a political comeback when she stood for a by-election in the Chikmagalur District of the southern state of Karnataka and won overwhelmingly. The Parliament eventually disqualified her from holding the seat: it judged her to be in contempt of Parliament and guilty of abusing Parliamentary privilege, because in 1975, when she was Prime Minister (a Parliamentary position), she had illegally used her office to quash an investigation of Sanjay and his car company. However, her election and her disqualification aroused great popular sympathy, and touched off demonstrations all over the country. This put additional pressure on Desai and Charan Singh to reach a modus vivendi.

In January, 1979, the cause of Janata Party unity finally prevailed, and a complicated formula for Charan Singh's return to the Cabinet was worked out. He was named Deputy Prime Minister, but his influence was somewhat reduced, for he came back not with his previous post of Home Affairs Minister—the portfolio second to that of the Prime Minister—but as Finance Minister, and Raj Narain, to whom Desai objected strongly, was not taken back. (His portfolio of Public Health was given to another of Charan Singh's allies, one Rabi Ray.) Jagjivan Ram was also given the title Deputy Prime Minister, but in protocol matters he was junior to Charan Singh. He felt, however, that he was in no position to protest, because his own influence had eroded somewhat—for familial reasons. His son Suresh, a middle-aged married man, had become involved in some unsavory sex scandals that could not be covered up. Besides, Jagjivan Ram was able to tell himself that his Defense Ministry was more powerful than Charan Singh's Finance Ministry, and that the Finance Ministry often becomes the scapegoat for a country's economic ills. Most important of all, the formula provided that Charan Singh was to have his way with the special courts, and also that the charges against both Desai's son and Charan Singh's sons-in-law were to be somehow investigated. Almost immediately, however, Charan Singh's special-court proposal was blocked by Mrs. Gandhi and her lawyers, who, in a delaying tactic, set about challenging its constitutionality in the courts. As for the investigation of Desai's and Charan Singh's families, Desai merely asked Y. V. Chandrachud, the Chief Justice of the Supreme Court, to conduct an informal investigation. Chandrachud declined; he felt that no sitting judge should be asked to take on such a controversial political problem, and anyway he did not see that an investigation could get anywhere without subpoena powers, which only a formally impanelled commission of inquiry or, of course, a law court was permitted. He suggested that a retired colleague, C. A. Vaidialingam, who needed something to do, look into the matter. Charan Singh, Desai, and Chandrachud all knew that recourse to Vaidialingam provided them with a discreet way of shelving the problem for the time being, and they agreed upon it.

Charan Singh's return to the Cabinet as senior Deputy Prime Minister was viewed as a stunning defeat for Desai, and Charan Singh, from the inside, and Raj Narain, from the outside, thereupon all but openly started a campaign to dethrone Desai, though publicly Charan Singh denied that he had any such design. As late as May, he said, "I am not a rival of Prime Minister Morarji Desai for either the Party leadership or the post of Prime Minister. Mr. Desai must and will remain the Prime Minister as long as he wishes. It was I who wanted Mr. Desai to be Prime Minister, and I will be the last person to do anything to remove him." Unexpectedly, Charan Singh's ambition to become Prime Minister received a lift from Mrs. Gandhi's camp. On June 25th, she ousted from her Congress Indira Party the chief minister of Karnataka, Devraj Urs, who had been one of her most powerful supporters through the post-Emergency period. Urs had long looked to Mrs. Gandhi to help him build up a national constituency, and Mrs. Gandhi had long looked to him to assure her of a solid power base in South India, which she might use for a return to office. (South India, by and large, had been spared the effects of the Emergency; the opposition to Mrs. Gandhi had been concentrated in North India, and so North India had taken the brunt of the Emergency's authoritarian measures. During the state elections in 1978, Urs had helped the Congress Indira Party to capture control of Karnataka and neighboring Andhra Pradesh.) But lately Urs, who had come increasingly to regard Sanjay as both Mrs. Gandhi's and Congress Indira's greatest political liability, had been pressing her to denounce Sanjay and put political distance between herself and her son. She had never recanted on the Emergency, and she had no intention of condemning her son. Urs now denounced her, saying, in a parting open letter, "We refuse to be treated as bonded labour. . . . You have learnt nothing from your experience and the authoritarian bent of your mind still persists, which is an anomaly in a democratic society. . . . You scare away all good, capable, and efficient men and women and then you hope to administer this vast nation with mediocres and sycophants." He put her on notice that he would call a convention of other Congress Indira critics, and he immediately became a rival for the loyalty of Congress Indira members in Karnataka and elsewhere who admired her but regarded her attachment to Sanjay as politically ruinous. With the departure of Urs, Mrs. Gandhi was left with the rump of the rump, and it was generally assumed that this time she was irreparably finished as a politician.

With Mrs. Gandhi no longer looming as a threat, the last inducement for the Janata leaders to work together had evaporated. On June 26th—just a day after the ouster of Urs—Raj Narain bolted the Janata Party. His was the first such move, and it was seen as an indication that within the Janata Party dissatisfaction with Desai's rule was widespread. Narain's defection, a symptom of a more general disintegration of governmental authority, came at a particularly difficult time for the country. In Gujarat, a dam had burst, and hundreds of people had drowned in a single day. In West Bengal, there was a severe epidemic of infectious hepatitis, and many people in Calcutta had died. In Delhi, sanitation workers who wanted more pay had sabotaged the city's water supply, and the water was unsafe to drink. Everywhere, inflation was worsening (the prices of coal, steel, cement, oil, electric power, and food were all going up), strikes among both workers and students were becoming routine, and the police were disobeying government orders. Essentially, the social and economic conditions in the country were reminiscent of those just before the Emergency. In addition, the country was suffering the worst drought of the century.

The Janata government had been in power for more than

two years and had accomplished little. But then the problems of the country were huge and were constantly growing. Over the years, it seemed, no government had been able to make much impression on them, with the result that whichever government happened to be in power was despised and always appeared inferior to the previous one. The outpouring of good will which had swept the Janata Party to power had long since been dissipated, and now that people had been saturated with the revelations of the "crimes and horrors of the Emergency" they had begun to sympathize with Mrs. Gandhi, and to look back even on the Emergency with yearning. Any government was better than no government—which was how the Janata government was increasingly seen. On July 12th, Charan Singh and Bahuguna, though they were arch-rivals in the Cabinet, expediently got together for the purpose of bringing down Desai. Charan Singh, Bahuguna, and many senior and junior Ministers resigned from the Cabinet and—along with all the members of the Bharatiya Lok Dal, among others—defected from the Janata Party, giving as their reason a charge that had often been made before: that Desai was promoting the chauvinist theocratic program of the right-wing Hindu nationalist Jana Sangh at the expense of the secular policies of the other constituent parties.

For many months, there had been growing violence against Untouchables and Muslims. In several places, upper-caste Hindus had burned down entire village areas where Untouchables lived, and elsewhere there had been Hindu-Muslim riots, as at the time of Partition, in 1947. The Jana Sangh had been linked to one particular Hindu-Muslim riot, in which at least a hundred and fifty people died. The Bharatiya Lok Dal defectors singled out the Jana Sangh's National Volunteer Corps—called Rashtriya Swayamsevak Sangh (R.S.S.) and sometimes referred to as the Jana Sangh's Brown Shirts—as the instigators of religious riots. It was true that some of the extremist members of the Jana Sangh sometimes talked as if they believed in Hitlerian theories of

Aryan supremacy. (Many Hindus in North India consider themselves descendants of Aryans, and consider the Untouchables and South Indians racially inferior.) It was also true that the Jana Sangh had significant influence both in the Janata government and in Desai's thinking. (His government had recently introduced a constitutional amendment to ban the killing of cows, and this amendment was seen as a Hindu attack on Muslims, since Hindus consider cows sacred, while Muslims eat beef.) Untouchables and Muslims had always been fearful of caste and religious persecution, and politicians had often played on these fears to win votes; actually, the so-called depressed classes—that is, the Untouchables and the very poor—and the religious minorities had formed Mrs. Gandhi's most loyal constituency, and in her political career she had often conjured up to great effect the bogey of the Jana Sangh and the R.S.S. But the Bharatiya Lok Dal defectors had all belonged to the Janata Party and the Janata government, and their making an issue of Jana Sangh influence at this particular time was seen as a bid to lay claim to Mrs. Gandhi's old constituency even as they undermined Desai's government—a cunning opportunistic ploy to isolate Mrs. Gandhi and Desai at a stroke and so seize power. Indeed, Charan Singh and his lieutenant Raj Narain immediately founded a new party, which they named Janata Secular.

On the day of the defections, Yeshwantrao Balwantrao Chavan, the head of the Official Congress Party, introduced a motion of no confidence in Desai's government, and a vote was scheduled for July 16th—four days later. On the fifteenth, George Fernandes, the Minister of Industries and the leader of the Socialist Party, resigned from the Cabinet, on the ground that Desai had lost the confidence of the Parliament and was now only clinging to his office. More defections from the Janata Party followed. Some of the defectors declared themselves independents, and others formed a socialist caucus, but many of them, sensing that Charan Singh might be the next Prime Minister, joined Janata Secular.

Defections and splits had been a way of life in state legislative assemblies ever since Independence, giving rise to the saying *"Aya Ram, gaya Ram"* ("Ram came, Ram went"), and had made state governments as unstable as the constantly shifting party loyalties of the legislators. Since 1963, defections and splits had become a way of life in Parliament as well. With each new defection and split, parties had lost their raisons d'être. This meant that all parties had ended up having no ideology, no body of convictions—no programs or principles to speak of—and that political contests had increasingly become vicious conflicts among personalities. Bills to discourage or ban defections—by making state legislators and members of Parliament at least serve out their terms with the party under whose aegis they had been elected—were often introduced in legislative assemblies and in Parliament, but they got nowhere, because initially the process of defection worked in the interests of a ruling party, as people were induced to cross over to it to get influence and power. It was when elections approached that defections and splits worked against it, as people scrambled to dissociate themselves from its failures. Parties therefore usually encouraged defections between elections but campaigned against them at election time.

Rather than face the humiliation of certain defeat in the Parliament, Desai—on the day of Fernandes' defection—resigned as Prime Minister. It was clear that, for the first time since Independence, no party had a majority in the Parliament, and that the only way to forestall its dissolution—something that no M.P. wanted, because an M.P. could not collect his pension unless he had served a full five-year term—was to form a coalition government. There followed the most unprincipled bit of horse-trading ever seen in the Indian Parliament. On July 18th, President Neelam Sanjiva Reddy called on Chavan to form a government, publicly explaining that Chavan had introduced the no-confidence motion and that it was in keeping with the highest democratic tradition to invite the leader of the opposition party to form a government. Technically, he should have called on a member of Congress Indira, which, with seventy-one seats, had recently replaced the Official Congress Party, with sixty-eight, as the chief opposition, the Official Congress having been weakened by defections. But Congress Indira, which was completely under the thumb of Mrs. Gandhi, even though she had been ousted from the Parliament, was deemed to have no chance of forming a coalition with any party. Chavan tried to woo various defecting groups to his side, but on July 22nd he told Reddy that he had been unable to form a government. He recommended that Charan Singh be asked next, declaring that he and his party were prepared to serve in Charan Singh's government. (It was odd that the members of the Official Congress Party, tainted, as they were, by their part in the Emergency, should be recommending Charan Singh, the member of the Janata government who had been the Emergency's most strident critic, for the Prime Ministership, but it was said that Charan Singh had offered to make Chavan Deputy Prime Minister if he himself succeeded in becoming Prime Minister.) Some of the Ministers, loyal to the Janata Party, pressed Desai to step down as Party leader in favor of Jagjivan Ram, who it was thought could preëmpt the support of the Official Congress Party from Charan Singh (Jagjivan Ram enjoyed much greater support among the rank and file of the Official Congress, because of his old connection with it), attract defectors from other parties, and, at the same time, hold together the remnants of the Janata Party. Anyway, these Ministers felt that, with party loyalties so fluid, whoever was first asked to form the new government would have the best chance of winning supporters by means of favors and promises. But Desai refused to make way for Jagjivan Ram, and the representation of Jagjivan Ram's Congress for Democracy was too small for him to do anything on his own, especially given the ingrained prejudice against Untouchables among the Jana Sangh members.

Desai insisted that he still had the most support in the Parliament, and that he should be given the chance to form a government. Charan Singh insisted that by now *he* had the most support, and that *he* should be given that chance. Reddy asked the two men to prove their competing claims by submitting lists of their committed supporters. Charan Singh's list turned out to have a few more bona-fide supporters than Desai's, and he won, but his list had a strange aspect. He came up with two hundred and thirty-eight names, among which were not only many members of the Official Congress Party, including Chavan, but also, surprisingly, the seventy-one members of Congress Indira. Under Indian law, Mrs. Gandhi was free to join Charan Singh's Cabinet, even though she was not a member of Parliament, provided she got herself elected to Parliament within six months of becoming a Minister. Yet Charan Singh had been decrying her villainy for years, and the failure of Desai to prosecute her had ostensibly been the main reason for Charan Singh's defection and for the fall of Desai's government. Even stranger was a declaration by Charan Singh when he submitted the list that he had not made Mrs. Gandhi any promises and, in fact, would not permit any member of her party to serve in his Cabinet. But this declaration rang hollow. Mrs. Gandhi had kept her independence of action, while he had lost his, for he could stay in power only as long as she supported him; his unrelenting effort to put her behind bars had culminated in his becoming her political hostage.

On July 27th, Desai finally resigned as the leader of the Janata Party, in favor of Jagjivan Ram—when Jagjivan Ram had lost his chance for the Prime Ministership to Charan Singh. In high moral dudgeon, Desai announced that he was leaving politics permanently, and gave as his reason the fact that the list of supporters he submitted to Reddy had accidentally contained the names of some members of the Official Congress Party, and that it was his "moral duty to atone for the lapse." Since the integrity of his list was of little consequence now that he had lost the murky battle, his self-righteous pronouncement could have been intended only to underscore the moral depravity of Charan Singh, Chavan, and Mrs. Gandhi.

On July 28th, Charan Singh was appointed Prime Minister, and he set about putting together a Cabinet. Of course, it was one thing for politicians to lend their names to a mere list of signatures and quite another for them to join the Cabinet, where, in helping Charan Singh rule, they might be tarnished by that rule. That same day, Charan Singh announced his Cabinet, and six of his fifteen Ministers proved to be from the Official Congress Party. The six could not be sworn in immediately, though, because of a rebellion among rank-and-file Party members, some of whom charged that the leaders had sold out the interests of the Party in return for Ministerial plums for themselves. The six were, however, sworn in on July 30th, having mollified the Party malcontents by promising them greater power in the Party. All six had been followers of Mrs. Gandhi, and five of them had served in her Cabinet right up until her 1977 defeat, but since then four of them had recanted on the Emergency and, by giving testimony against her before the Shah Commission, had helped to indict her and Sanjay on many charges that were now before the courts. And—just as had been rumored—Chavan, the star post-Emergency turncoat, had been named Deputy Prime Minister. Mrs. Gandhi claimed to be incensed, and announced that her Congress Indira was no longer under any obligation to support Charan Singh. This meant that (unless she changed her mind again) he would lose the vote of confidence that, in the normal course of things, followed on the heels of the formation of a Cabinet. Thus, within four days Mrs. Gandhi had succeeded in derailing Desai, together with Jagjivan Ram, then had helped make Charan Singh Prime Minister, and had now put herself in a position to derail Charan Singh.

Charan Singh's government and the Janata Secular Party— its president was Raj Narain—did not seem very different from Desai's government and the Janata Party. Some members of Parliament supported Charan Singh's government on the ground that they wanted to lessen political dependence on the "authoritarian forces" associated first with Mrs. Gandhi's Emergency government and later with Desai's government; other members of Parliament stayed out of Charan Singh's government on the ground that it was dependent on the same "authoritarian forces" as Mrs. Gandhi's Emergency government. Some members supported Charan Singh's government on the ground that they wanted to fight caste oppression and religious violence; other members stayed out of Charan Singh's government on the ground that it, like Desai's, was rooted in caste and religious politics. Some members supported it on the ground that it was committed to strengthening the central government and arresting the spread of anarchy, while other members supported it on the ground that it would weaken the central government and so promote greater democracy. One leading member announced that he was joining the new government because of Charan Singh's public espousal of the notion of special courts; another leading member announced that he was joining the new government because Charan Singh had privately abandoned the notion of special courts, as antithetical to the spirit of democracy. But if it was hard to make out what particular principle, policy, or program was at stake, Charan Singh had finally realized an often stated ambition—"to go down in history as a Prime Minister of India."

Charan Singh did not immediately go to the Parliament for a vote of confidence; because he needed to shore up his support, the President gave him an unusual three-week grace period, until August 20th. Charan Singh at once busied himself looking for a quid pro quo that Mrs. Gandhi might accept as a price for her renewed support, and also bargaining with still loyal members of the Janata Party to get them to defect to his side. All the negotiations were conducted in the all-or-nothing atmosphere of a poker game. If Charan Singh failed to get a vote of confidence, the President could call on Jagjivan Ram and give him a chance to form a government or he could equally well dissolve the Parliament.

The lengths to which Charan Singh was prepared to go were made unmistakably clear by one of his appointments: he named Bahuguna as his Finance Minister. At this time, Charan Singh's April, 1978, letter to Desai attacking Bahuguna surfaced—along with a similar letter from Bahuguna to Desai attacking Charan Singh—so on August 11th, in the middle of the grace period, Charan Singh and Bahuguna issued a joint statement, which went, in part:

> Our disagreements over various national issues in the past are well-known. We may have some differences in these areas even now. But they are more of emphasis than of a basic nature. So far as misunderstanding between us in evaluating each other is concerned, we have found common ground and complete understanding has replaced the earlier misunderstanding. The Jana Sangh and the R.S.S. were and are a common enemy to both of us. . . . We have realized that there is a compelling need to forge a common front to fight the fascist forces, represented by those who believe in the Hitlerian theory of ethnic purism, religious supremacy and bigotry. . . . We appeal to all secular and democratic forces wherever they are to rise above personal considerations and conventional norms in this great task of taking Indian democracy to a new phase of secular consolidation and egalitarian justice to the urban and the rural poor, the Harijans [Untouchables], the Adivasis [tribal people], and the minorities.

Later, Charan Singh sent a letter to Bahuguna saying that he was sorry to have given the impression that Bahuguna was a K.G.B. agent. He went on to assert that the charge was originally made by Desai, and that he was only repeating it in his April letter to Desai. Desai immediately denied Charan Singh's assertion. The response of Bahuguna—who, for his part, had once called Charan Singh a "mentally deranged person"—is not known.

As late as August 19th, Charan Singh was meeting with Mrs. Gandhi in an attempt to regain her support. On that day, Raj Narain went as far as to meet for an hour and a half with Sanjay. Then Charan Singh announced that Mrs. Gandhi's support for his Cabinet was "unconditional." At the same time, he appointed two new Ministers to placate other groups—as if that support were in reality anything but "unconditional." All in all, he gave the impression that he was jittery about the vote of confidence the next day.

On August 20th, Mrs. Gandhi, who had held her cards close to her chest up to the last possible moment, announced that her party would not vote for Charan Singh's Cabinet after all. Charan Singh and his Cabinet resigned without facing the vote of confidence (the two new Ministers had held office for less than twenty-four hours), and Charan Singh was forced to do a complete about-turn. He issued a statement in which—contradicting his announcement of the day before—he claimed that Mrs. Gandhi had laid down numerous conditions before consenting to give him her support, and that these conditions had been unacceptable. In particular, he accused her of trying to blackmail him in the matter of the establishment of the special courts. "The country would not have forgiven us if we had, for the sake of remaining in office, agreed to withdraw prosecutions against persons responsible for atrocities during the Emergency and for subjecting thousands of innocent people and families to cruel sufferings and harassment," he declared. "By temperament, I would not have liked to continue in power even for a day yielding to blackmail of this type and would rather be with the people and fight along with them to strengthen the basic values of democracy, secularism, and socialism."

During the three-week grace period, Mrs. Gandhi's popular appeal had climbed dramatically. It had not stood so high since before the Emergency. Her opponents had been shown up as unprincipled and self-serving, in line with the widespread view that this was in the nature of politics. If everyone in politics acted in an unprincipled and self-serving way, then what she had done did not seem so reprehensible—politics was merely a game, which had nothing to do with society at large.

Charan Singh's formal letter of resignation to the President stated:

MY DEAR RASHTRAPATIJI [Respected Father of the Nation, as the President is called],
The Cabinet met this morning and took a decision as follows:
"We had formed the Government with a view to restoring effective democracy and secularism. We had further hoped that we would be able to bring light into the life of the deprived and the downtrodden, to restore confidence amongst the minorities and weaker sections which had badly been shaken especially during the previous regime. We regret, however, that communal and authoritarian forces have conspired to defeat our aims of building a society, by and large, based on the teaching of Gandhiji.
"The Cabinet, therefore, decides to resign. It further resolves to advice [sic] the President that in view of the present situation, arrangements should be made for a fresh mandate being obtained from the people."

In the light of the above, I hereby tender my resignation and that of my Council of Ministers.

Most of the M.P.s were stunned by the news of the possible dissolution of Parliament: not only would their pensions be in jeopardy but going to the electorate after little more than two years, and with not much to show for it, hardly augured well for their being returned to office. For the people at large, too, the news—except insofar as it promised the entertaining spectacle of an election—was unwelcome: during the months of campaigning, the government would come to a standstill, and, besides, elections were too expensive to be held so frequently. But how much latitude the President had on whether to follow or to ignore the advice of Charan Singh and his Cabinet was a moot question. Charan Singh and his Cabinet insisted that the President was only a figurehead and, under the Parliamentary form of government, was bound to follow their advice. Jagjivan Ram and the president of the Janata Party, Chandra Shekhar, took the contrary position. They called on President Reddy and told him that Charan Singh and his Cabinet, since they had never faced a vote of confidence, had no authority to recommend the dissolution of Parliament. After all, as President he had exercised his discretion by calling first on Chavan and then on Charan Singh to form a government, and he should now complete the logical process by calling on Jagjivan Ram to do the same.

The President thereupon began a series of secret consultations with various party leaders and legal authorities, ostensibly to determine what procedure he should follow. Almost all the party leaders—except, of course, the leaders of the Janata—advised dissolution, for their own reasons: Charan Singh because, having been unable to form an acceptable government, he did not want anyone else to; Mrs. Gandhi because she hoped to overturn the verdict of the 1977 elections; the leaders of the smaller parties because, as always, they hoped to gain at the expense of the larger parties. Legal authorities on the constitution, however, contended that to dissolve a Parliament without any government's having lost a vote of confidence, and without the President's having given the leader of the largest party—in this case, Jagjivan Ram—a chance to form a government, was to go against both the letter and the spirit of the constitution. The President's problem was compounded by the obvious fact that Jagjivan Ram could form a government only by means of further defections and re-defections, and a government made up of defectors was inherently unstable. It was hardly surprising that when Jagjivan Ram was questioned on how he would form a government he equivocated. On August 21st, the *Statesman* reported, "Asked whether the government he proposed to form would be a coalition or a single-party one, Mr. Jagjivan Ram said: 'It may be both.' " There was also an imponderable personal factor in the President's decision. In 1969, Reddy's ambition to become the President of India had been thwarted by Jagjivan Ram, who, siding with Mrs. Gandhi, had denied him the prize just when it seemed to be within his reach. (Reddy had, of course, become President only after Mrs. Gandhi's 1977 defeat.) Now that Reddy was in a position to thwart Jagjivan Ram's ambition, would he pay him in kind, or forgive and forget?

On August 22nd, the President announced that he was dissolving the Parliament. This meant that until after the election Charan Singh and his Cabinet would rule as a caretaker government, enjoying the benefits of incumbency.

The *Statesman* explained the next day:

> What tilted the scales against the Janata leader was Mrs. Gandhi's decision to join almost all the other parties in demanding a mid-term election. Since Mr. Jagjivan Ram could not muster an absolute majority, he could have won a confidence vote in the Lok Sabha [the lower house] only on

the strength of defectors who would join him and his party for a price, leading to further debasement of political and moral values.

The constitutional aspects of the President's decision will no doubt be debated at length, but it is important to bear in mind that the essence of the practice of parliamentary democracy and the ideals that guided the framers of our Constitution were being blatantly negated by almost all the parties. The nation has, indeed, faced a total crisis of leadership in which men and women who had won the respect and, up to a point, admiration of the people showed themselves to be unprincipled power-hungry persons interested only in satisfying their own appetites.

. . . Politicians of most of the parties have only themselves to blame for creating conditions which have been effectively, if cynically, exploited by Mrs. Gandhi to rehabilitate herself and humiliate two Prime Ministers.

Indian politicians are notorious for being bad losers, and Reddy had hardly finished making his announcement before Chandra Shekhar and Jagjivan Ram set up a hue and cry for his impeachment. They accused Reddy of being anti-Janata, anti-Jagjivan Ram, anti-Untouchable. (Some of the members of the Janata Party were circulating a rumor that the Russians had given Reddy ten million rupees because they wanted Mrs. Gandhi, who was known for her pro-Soviet policies, to come back to power.) In a joint statement reported in the papers on August 23rd, the two men said:

> The course of events over the past month as well as the sudden decision of the President testify to a deep conspiracy. . . .
>
> If this decision is allowed to stand our country will have no safeguards left against Presidential arbitrariness and against the fact that a President may be propelled to such arbitrary action by blackmail or by other inducements. Al-

ready, the way has been opened for a Presidential dictatorship.

Chandra Shekhar went as far as to say that the President's single action was worse than Mrs. Gandhi's Emergency. The claim was patently absurd; after all, the President had not muzzled the press, arrested anyone, or traduced the judiciary. The *Hindustan Times* was moved to comment in an editorial:

> Mr. Chandra Shekhar and others like him are not only not in jail but free to participate actively in politics and speak their minds. The press has no difficulty in reporting them. The judiciary remains free. The Constitution, which has been purged of some of the Emergency distortions, remains in unfettered operation. The oppressive climate of fear, which characterised the Emergency, is conspicuous by its absence. The allegation that the President's action has been worse than that of Mrs. Gandhi in the distortions it has wrought, therefore, does not bear scrutiny. Anyone who levels it runs the risk of undermining his own credibility. Far worse, it has the effect of projecting the Emergency as something far less grim and deplorable than it was. This can have very serious consequences when attempts to justify the Emergency have been launched on a large scale with an eye to the elections.

In the seventies, the Indian electorate had begun sending to Parliament a new breed of politicians, who might have accurately reflected the rustic character of the people they represented but who cut a strange figure in New Delhi. Most of these politicians had no profession or passion, hobby or interest other than winning votes and staying in power. Since politics was their only means of livelihood, they often had to make as much money as they could while they were in office in order to survive when they were out of office. Nevertheless, most of the charges of corruption they hurled at each other and each other's families were preposterous, and had no other purpose than to make political hay. Many Indian politicans, of course, have always tended to favor their relatives and friends for jobs or for the perquisites of power. But then it is not surprising that in a poor society people should favor a family member in need over a stranger in need, or a loyal child over a possibly treacherous acquaintance. Perhaps because of the imagined or real corruption everywhere, these new politicians, even as they clung to office, vied with one another to appear holier than thou. They tended to take up political issues like the banning of cow slaughter and the institution of prohibition. When the issues were not moral, they were parochial. (In one election, one party demanded a separate Ministry for films, because its head, the chief minister of the state of Tamil Nadu—formerly Madras—was the leading film actor of South India.) The issues might not have been wholly without merit, but the hypocrisy and bigotry that attended them contributed to the prevailing political mood of cynicism and futility.

Charan Singh and Raj Narain were not untypical of the new breed of politicians. Both had got their start in the faction-ridden parochial politics of Uttar Pradesh. Both had made a career of defecting from one splinter group to another in the name of sincerity and socialist revolution. (One of Raj Narain's favorite cries was "Change the government again and again!") Like Raj Narain, Charan Singh was often referred to as a "stormy petrol," because of his turbulent politics. Both talked as if politics were a religious struggle of mythic proportions. Raj Narain often spoke of Charan Singh as the incarnation of Rama, and of Charan Singh's wife as the incarnation of Rama's wife, Sita, just as he spoke of himself as the incarnation of the monkey-god Hanuman; in the Ramayana, Hanuman, with an army of monkeys, rescued Sita from the clutches of Rama's enemy, the demon Ravana. Raj Narain claimed that he grew up reciting the Chalisa—forty prayers in praise of Hanuman—and that he still said at least seven prayers a day in praise of him. He felt that, like Hanuman, he was leading an army—in his case, an army of politicians—to rescue the country from corruption and demons.

Charan Singh, who had been in political life for nearly forty years, made a career of being a malcontent—of swimming against the current, of taking contrary views, of responding negatively, and of bringing down governments and parties. (His resignation from Desai's government in 1979 was his eleventh resignation from office.) Somehow, his resignations always seemed to propel him to higher positions of power. (One of his nicknames was Chair Singh—"chair" having been a symbol of power in India since British times.) Charan Singh was born poor, and never quite stopped struggling—as if he could not forget his humble origins. He became a symbol of the Janata government's shift of emphasis from the development of Western-type industries, associated with the policies of Nehru and Mrs. Gandhi, to the development of indigenous agriculture, associated with the ideals of Mahatma Gandhi. "I am a man of old values," he liked to say, and he was so anti-Western that he refused to use soap, listen to the radio, or watch television. His approaches to India's problems tended to be extreme. At one time, he insisted that no work should be done by machines—that even safety matches, produced by machine in India, should be made by hand. On another occasion, he suggested that in order to break down caste barriers higher jobs in the civil service and the military should be open only to those who had married outside their caste. No one, however, doubted his sincerity; he was one politician who actually employed an Untouchable cook. He had always championed the Untouchables and the Muslims, but, because he had been a regional leader for most of his life, he had never acquired a national following in either community. Similarly, one of his oldest slogans was "peasant power," but since he belonged to the subcaste of Jats, more often than not "peasant power" had been interpreted by the public to mean "Jat power."

The hallmark of Raj Narain was his loose tongue. He once said of Jagjivan Ram, "He has so much money that if he does not spend it his stomach will burst." Whenever he was criticized, he would say things like "This tongue was given to me by God. How can you check me?" *India Today* wrote, "His continuous barrage of junk-talk—which has won him wide publicity and made some cynics compare his sayings to the utterances of Idi Amin—reduces him to a frequently painful caricature." Many people began avoiding him. (Once, when Desai returned to New Delhi from abroad, Raj Narain greeted him at the airport and sprayed him with perfume. Desai said to him, "You are applying perfume now, but in my absence your doings were spreading a foul smell.") After he helped to bring down Desai's government and install Charan Singh as Prime Minister in the caretaker government, he started calling himself "king-breaker and king-maker," "super-man," and "super-Prime Minister." *India Today* wrote, "His newly acquired eminence glows through his sweaty beard as he pats his garlands in place, pants across the runway to meet his followers, and waves his walking stick in universal approbation. Jokester and buffoon, toppler of two prime ministers, perpetual jack-in-the-box, the man has arrived."

Raj Narain, who had long since abandoned his family for celibacy, claimed that he had a celibate's devotion to what he considered public life. "A man who chooses public life should quit his private life," he once said. "How can you hope to be close to the *janata* if you hang on to your family?" In his new political life, old contradictions abounded. One day, he would describe Desai as the gift of God to India; another day, he would say, "He does not have a mind. How can he have a mental state?" One day, he would attack Mrs. Gandhi as the scourge of the nation; another day, he would praise her, saying, "There is a qualitative change between Mrs. Gandhi as Prime Minister and Mrs. Gandhi without the Prime Ministership." One day, he would describe Charan Singh as Rama incarnate; another day, he would attack him. He was a socialist who was also a Hindu fanatic. He was a universalist who was also a Hindu communalist. His ideology sounded like a hodgepodge of Sanskrit verses, Marxist homilies, and populist slogans. He claimed to believe that if people would unite they could bring about a world government without disparity either of income or of class, and with no need for passports or visas. He said that such a world government would be run by a Parliament like India's and by leaders like him. He claimed to believe that such an ideal order had existed in India in some ancient time—when politics and science were so advanced that surgeons could mount elephants' heads on human bodies, as in the pictures of the god Ganesh. "Nowadays, even the most advanced surgeons can only transplant hearts," he said. No one was ever sure whether Raj Narain was expressing a genuine belief or saying something merely to attract attention. In 1979, a well-known Bombay film comedian and amateur wrestler, I. S. Johar, apparently felt that Raj Narain had turned Indian politics into a joke. He challenged him to a wrestling bout to decide which one of them was better qualified to sit in Parliament. At the same time, he announced that he would stand from whichever constituency Raj Narain chose to represent in the coming elections, and that all the comedians in Indian films would campaign for him against Narain. Johar said that his slogan would be "My name is Joker." In the end, Johar, hedging his bets, stood from both Delhi and Bombay, and Raj Narain stood from Benares. Both lost.

During the election campaign of 1979–80, it sometimes seemed that India was back in the days before the British raj, when rajas and maharajas fought with each other by fair means or foul—with this difference: the rajas and maharajas used foot soldiers and fought for supremacy over separate slices of the country, while the new "princes" used promises and fought for supremacy over the whole of India. It often seemed that the social and economic consensus that had ruled India since Independence—except during the period of the Emergency—had now broken down. (Some commentators consoled themselves with the thought that worse things were happening in Muslim countries to the west.) In the elections, a total of four thousand six hundred and eight candidates stood for five hundred and twenty-five seats. (Actually, the lower house has five hundred and forty-two seats, but in the northeast and in other places voting was postponed indefinitely because of political violence.) For the first time, more than half the candidates stood as independents—a change reflecting the general breakdown of parties. There were three hundred and fifty-four million eligible voters, many of whom lived in remote villages. Informing them about the issues and recording their votes was no easy task; a candidate had to drum into the voters' heads the symbol assigned to him or his party. The spectacle of the election campaign, therefore, had the aspect of a desultory national festival lasting more than four months.

Seventy per cent of the voters could neither read nor write. The ballot was mostly a roster of symbols, and people voted by marking with a rubber stamp the symbols of the candidates or parties of their choice. Established, familiar symbols were so important that splinter groups fought over them, and often the symbols had to be replaced or altered. At one time, there was only one symbol of any consequence—the Congress Party's two yoked bullocks. That symbol, being associated with the names of Mahatma Gandhi and Nehru, automatically got most of the votes. But with the proliferation of parties and splinter groups the old symbols were robbed of their traditional associations, and a bewildering number of new symbols appeared: a hammer and sickle with stars; a hammer and sickle without stars;

a hammer; a sickle; a peasant with a bullock; a peasant with a plow; a bullock; a bullock cart; a plow; a bird; a tree; a fish; a bicycle. Moreover, the symbol of a party sometimes changed from election to election: in the 1977 elections, Mrs. Gandhi's party symbol was a cow and a calf (the symbol gave rise to some mirth because of its connection with mother and son); in the 1980 elections, it was the palm of a hand.

During the 1979–80 campaign, the candidates of Janata and the Lok Dal (Charan Singh and Raj Narain had changed their splinter party's name from Janata Secular to Lok Dal) either attacked each other or, in the manner of the proverbial generals who are always fighting the last war, attacked the Emergency. Yet they did not succeed, as they had during the 1977 election campaign, in besmirching Mrs. Gandhi with the scandal of Sanjay, who was again standing for election from Amethi. The editor of the *Statesman,* S. Nihal Singh, explained this failure by writing, "Sons of politicians, peddling influence or making money on the side, have ceased to surprise voters." Indeed, many of the Janata and Lok Dal candidates were relatives of public figures: there was the wife of Charan Singh, a daughter-in-law of Jagjivan Ram, and even a sister-in-law of Jaya Prakash Narayan, who had died in October of 1979, at the age of seventy-six. (In Srinagar, the capital of Kashmir, the National Conference candidate, Farooq Abdullah, was the son of the chief minister, Sheikh Mohammed Abdullah, and he was declared the winner before the formal balloting, because no one came forward to oppose him.)

Mrs. Gandhi, using a chartered Viscount plane supplemented by three helicopters, travelled more than anyone else, penetrating deep into the interior of the country and covering a total of forty thousand miles. She made at least twenty speeches a day, and, according to some estimates, she was seen by almost a hundred million people. She hardly referred to the Emergency, and instead concentrated on two up-to-the-minute themes: the prices of three necessities—kerosene, sugar, and onions—which, in part because of the jump in world oil prices and in part because of the 1979 drought, had risen precipitously during Charan Singh's regime; and the breakdown of law and order ("Today, law-abiding citizens are afraid of ruffians, thieves, and murderers, and criminals aren't afraid of anyone"), which, in part because of deteriorating economic and political conditions, had become widespread during Charan Singh's regime. She portrayed her opponents as bumbling, weak, vain, quarrelsome old men, and presented herself as the only person capable of giving the country a strong government. Everywhere she went, she raised the palm of her hand in salute, and asked people to put their rubber stamp on the palm-of-a-hand symbol on the ballot. (To some observers, the symbol of the saluting hand conjured up the Nazis, especially since the stamp that Indians use for voting is a swastika. But in India raising a hand is an ancient salutation, and the swastika remains the ancient symbol of the sun.) She was helped in her campaign by several circumstances: the Janata and Lok Dal candidates who had served in Parliament had arrogantly neglected to keep in touch with their constituencies; Charan Singh frequently delivered himself of atavistic pronouncements against industrialism and Western values, which alienated the urban intelligentsia; and, what was perhaps most important, Charan Singh's government repeatedly delayed the elections. The official reason for the delays was that the large number of parties and groups made it difficult to organize the balloting; the unofficial reason was that the Lok Dal was making a poor showing in the country, and its leaders regretted having precipitated the elections in the first place. Raj Narain even intimated that the government might cancel the elections, because of anarchic conditions in the country—an argument straight out of the Emergency book. Whatever the reason for the delays, they gave Mrs. Gandhi many months in which to dramatize the impotence of a government without her at the helm, and to blur the distinction between Desai's and Charan Singh's governments. She had more money (businessmen tired of strikes and indiscipline in the factories apparently contributed heavily to her campaign), better organization (she is renowned for her skill in managing party affairs), and certainly more energy than many of her opponents, and she succeeded in getting herself across.

When it began to look as if Mrs. Gandhi had a chance of capturing a substantial number of seats in the Parliament, a half-dozen Ministers from Charan Singh's government defected to her party, among them K. Brahmananda Reddy (no relation of President Reddy), who had served as her Home Affairs Minister during the Emergency; then, after her 1977 defeat, had parted company with her; then had precipitated the 1978 split of the Congress Party, which resulted in her founding the Congress Indira; and, finally, had become Minister of Industries in Charan Singh's government—continually giving the impression that his latest change was his last. But the *Statesman* noted:

> Mr. Reddy . . . is not alone in changing sides more than once after having created the impression that the first change was irrevocable. Mr. Bahuguna left the Congress for Janata, ratted on the latter to join hands with Mr. Charan Singh, and then re-ratted to return to [Mrs. Gandhi's] fold which he had earlier found too authoritarian for his democratic conscience.

No sooner had Bahuguna returned than Mrs. Gandhi made him the secretary-general of her party and the manager of her campaign, no doubt because he was one of the leading pro-Muslim politicians in India and so was able to mobilize the Muslim vote for her. (Soon after his defection-to her side, she received the endorsement of the Imam of the Great Mosque in Delhi, who had denounced her and the Emergency at the time of the 1977 election campaign and had thus cost her valuable Muslim support.) Even Mrs. Gandhi's prosecutors rushed to join her.

One was Amrit Nahata, who after the 1977 elections had brought the celebrated suit against Sanjay and Sanjay's associates for the theft and destruction of his film "Kissa Kursi Ka." On Nahata's testimony, Sanjay had been convicted in February of 1979, sentenced to two years of "rigorous imprisonment," and jailed—but only briefly. He was free to campaign while his conviction was under appeal to the Supreme Court. During the election campaign, Nahata did a complete about-face, claiming, in a petition to the Supreme Court, that he had given false testimony in the case, and that Charan Singh had put him up to it. Charan Singh responded by saying, "If Mr. Nahata was in desperate search for an excuse to join Mrs. Gandhi's party, he should have discovered one which would not have exposed him as a self-condemned liar." In any event, the race was clearly narrowing down to a one-woman show—a process that was hastened when Charan Singh tried to taint Jagjivan Ram with the charge of being a C.I.A. agent, much as he (or Desai) had earlier tried to taint Bahuguna with the charge of being a K.G.B. agent. Charan Singh's new charge grew out of statements, in Henry Kissinger's memoirs and in Thomas Powers' biography of Richard Helms, that the United States had had a plant in Mrs. Gandhi's Cabinet who in the days preceding the 1971 India-Pakistan war fed information to the Nixon Administration about the Indians' plan to dismember Pakistan. But the charge, because it pitted Jagjivan Ram against Charan Singh, only succeeded in strengthening Mrs. Gandhi's hand.

In January, 1980, Mrs. Gandhi was returned to power as swiftly and decisively as she had been swept out of it. She carried with her Sanjay and many of his young followers; in fact, all those of his followers who stood for Parliament were elected.

5

Intimations of
a Nehru Dynasty

Though all the portents pointed to a victory for Mrs. Gandhi, when it came everyone was surprised by its size. The dumbfounded Jagjivan Ram said, "It's either magic or a miracle." Three hundred and fifty-one of the five hundred and twenty-five M.P.s elected to the lower house were from Congress Indira. Although Charan Singh and Jagjivan Ram were returned, many other opposition stalwarts were defeated, and not one of the minority parties won even the fifty seats necessary to qualify as the official opposition. (Actually, the Communist parties collectively did better than any of the others.) Without imposing any constraints or countervailing balances on Mrs. Gandhi's power, the voters presented her with a blank check.

Most of the newly elected M.P.s of Congress Indira were inexperienced; two out of three had never served in Parliament before. Few of them had independently earned a position of respect; their only recommendation was their youth. It was reported that as many as a hundred and fifty of them had been handpicked by Sanjay, and were therefore beholden only to him. (They referred to him as Raj Kumar, or Crown Prince.) As it happened, these elections made Sanjay one of the first of the "sons of politicians" ever to sit in Parliament. He certainly did his mother one better: she had not sat in Parliament in her father's lifetime. Further, the elections returned all the members of the Sanjay Caucus, including Bansi Lal, who, as the Defense Minister during the Emergency, had been Sanjay's greatest promoter in the Army, and V. C. Shukla, who, as the Minister of Information and Broadcasting during the Emergency, had been the architect of its press censorship. The inevitable post mortems followed: it was said that the vote was unrepresentative (only a hundred and ninety-six million, or not much more than half of those eligible, voted) and that the general apathy worked in Mrs. Gandhi's favor, since her supporters were enthusiastic and went to the polls, while her opponents' supporters were lukewarm and stayed away from the polls; that the vote was more against Desai and Charan Singh than for Mrs. Gandhi; that the vote was swung by the price of onions—the *sine qua non* of Indian cooking—and so on. All the same, Mrs. Gandhi's party received only forty-two and a half per cent of the popular vote, and was able to chalk up its huge victory in part because her Janata and Lok Dal opponents drew votes away from each other, so that they all went down to defeat.

Mrs. Gandhi's assessment of the election results was frankly grandiose. She dismissed the whole Desai and Charan Singh period as an aberration, saying of the voters, "They woke up in 1977, soon after making their big mistake"—as if in the three intervening years they had only been waiting to put her back in office. When she announced her Cabinet, Sanjay was not given a post, and this made some observers think that she would move cautiously. Immediately upon coming to office, she took a pro-Soviet stand on the invasion of Afghanistan, and this made other observers think that she would move boldly. Within a few days, however, she backed away from her pro-Soviet stand, only to reverse herself again, and this made still other observers think that she would vacillate. Soon such speculations simmered down, as there were signs that the mother and son were tilting toward some form of authoritarianism; they injected elements of fear and propaganda into the political climate. Mrs. Gandhi's government, among other things, began hitting the supposed enemies of Sanjay in the civil service and the police. For instance, it summarily removed N. K. Singh, of the Central Bureau of Investigation, who was in charge of the court cases in the Bureau arising out of the Emergency, and dispatched him for "interrogation" to the state of Haryana after its government defected to Congress Indira. Since it was N. K. Singh who had made the argument against Sanjay and won his conviction in the case of the "Kissa Kursi Ka" film, his removal was widely interpreted as the opening step in a campaign of personal vendetta to be waged by Sanjay. At the same time, Mrs. Gandhi's government restored passports to all the prominent Emergency suspects and started singling out Sanjay's friends and aides for special promotions. It leapfrogged over many senior officials to appoint two post-Emergency pariahs, Jag Mohan and P. S. Bhinder, as Delhi's lieutenant governor and commissioner of police, respectively—making them perhaps the capital's two most important local officials. (During the Emergency, Jag Mohan, as the vice-chairman of the Delhi Development Authority, and Bhinder, as Delhi's deputy inspector general of police, had helped Sanjay carry out the notorious Operation Bulldozer, in which several hundred poor people's houses were demolished in the Turkman Gate area of the city as part of Sanjay's "national beautification program." Both Mohan and Bhinder had later been unsuccessfully prosecuted on a charge of ordering the murder of Sunder, Sanjay's ex-chum, when he was in police custody.) Mrs. Gandhi at first delayed the assigning of many important Ministerial portfolios—those of Defense; Industries; Labor; Planning; Public Health; Steel and Mines; and Petroleum, Chemicals, and Fertilizers—thus giving rise to speculation that she intended either to distribute the plums to her still unrewarded Emergency supporters once she had consolidated her power or to keep most of the strings of power in her own hands. (As it turned out, she did some of both.)

The 1980 elections were held only for the lower house of Parliament; the upper house and a majority of the total of twenty-two state assemblies, which elect many of the members of the upper house, remained under the opposition's control. Sanjay apparently advised his mother to use the momentum of her victory to dissolve the assemblies in states where she had a good chance of winning, and call early elections in those states. In February, she dissolved nine state assemblies that were under Janata and Lok Dal control but still had more or less functioning governments, on the ground that because of her victory they no longer represented the voters. (She did not tamper with the states that were controlled by Communists, because her party stood little chance of winning them.) Opposition politicians cried foul and claimed that her action was "antidemocratic," "autocratic," and "dictatorial." Charan Singh went as far as to say, "Fascism is on the prowl again." But the cries of Charan Singh and others sounded a little hollow, since they had followed the same strategy when they took control of the lower house in the 1977 elections. In May, Mrs. Gandhi's party won in eight of the nine contested states. This gave her control of both houses. In time, she came to enjoy control of sixteen of the twenty-two states—near-absolute power to do anything she pleased, just as at the time of the Emergency.

The election laid to rest all those court cases against mother and son which had preoccupied and paralyzed the governments of both Desai and Charan Singh; one of Mrs. Gandhi's former defense lawyers became her Law Minister. For a time, it seemed that Mrs. Gandhi might use Charan Singh's special courts to prosecute Charan Singh's and Desai's families. After months of investigation, Vaidialingam had surprised everyone by submitting a five-hundred-page report to Mrs. Gandhi's government in which he recommended a formal investigation of Charan

Singh's wife, of Kantilal, and of Kantilal's wife. The report charged, for instance, that Charan Singh's wife had received "fairly large amounts" of money from well-to-do young people in return for promises that she would help them find jobs; that Kantilal had generally assumed "extra-constitutional powers and authority over the governmental machinery for perpetrating and aggrandizing self-interests;" and that Kantilal's wife had pushed tax authorities around for personal gain. But nothing came of these charges against the families of Mrs. Gandhi's two predecessors. After all, Sanjay was in line to become one of his mother's Ministers—and the Prime Minister one day. Indeed, on June 13th she gave a public signal that he would probably succeed her: she made him a general secretary of Congress Indira, a Party post just below her own. By that time, her government was being spoken of as a "transition" to Sanjay's rule.

Shortly after seven o'clock on the morning of June 23rd, Sanjay came out of the Prime Minister's residence, at 1 Safdarjang Road, and got behind the wheel of his car—a green Matador, which is an Indian version of the Volkswagen bus. He drove to the Delhi Flying Club, about half a mile away, where the young and chic well-to-do go to sport with planes. There he met a friend, Captain Subhash Saxena, whom he invited to go up in his Pitts with him. Sanjay had recently acquired a Pitts S-2A, a two-seater, two-hundred-horsepower, light, aerobatic American plane. It was the only one of its kind in India and the star of the club's fleet of small planes. Saxena, who was a flying instructor at the club, demurred, saying that he shouldn't fly, because he might be going in for a hernia operation any day. But Sanjay wanted someone with him at the controls, and prevailed upon Saxena to go up. As they were walking toward the hangar where the plane—red, sleek, and new-looking—was housed, they were intercepted by the club's chief instructor, a Captain Shamim, who suggested that Sanjay go up in an Indian Pushpak with a flying trainee instead of taking up the Pitts with Saxena. The Pushpak was an old club standby, which Sanjay had flown innumerable times, while the Pitts had been in service only a few days. Sanjay himself had flown it for six of the ten hours it had been in the air, and he was very keen on it. But it was a tricky piece of equipment, and flying it required special training and experience. "I have to take up this red bird today," Sanjay said. "It's Pitts day."

The senior deputy director of the Civil Aviation Department, Mr. G. R. Kathpalia, had made a point of personally supervising the arrangements for Sanjay's flights since Mrs. Gandhi's return to power; junior officials in the department generally steered clear of Sanjay, for fear that they would be blamed if anything happened to him. Sanjay had a reputation for being something of a daredevil. Once, he had brought down a plane in a town that had no airport; another time, he had performed a particularly dangerous stunt—swooping down, without releasing the landing gear, until he was flying just a few feet off the ground, and then zooming up again. Kathpalia was now on hand as the Pitts was got ready, and he watched Sanjay and Saxena board the plane and strap themselves into the two seats. They received clearance from the control tower and took off. It was two minutes to eight.

The Pitts climbed rapidly and headed toward Willingdon Crescent, near the Prime Minister's residence. When it was about a thousand feet up, it attempted a stall turn. A stall turn—a quick, somersaultlike reversal—is considered advisable in a Pitts only for experienced Pitts pilots and at a height of not less than fifteen hundred feet. The Pitts banked, pitched, nosedived, spun, and crashed in a cluster of trees, just missing some barracks behind Willingdon Crescent. Both Sanjay and Saxena died instantly.

Mrs. Gandhi was at the site of the accident within minutes, and she accompanied the bodies to a nearby hospital, where eight surgeons worked almost five hours to prepare Sanjay's body for public viewing. They also embalmed the body—although the practice is unknown among Hindus—because Rajiv was vacationing in Italy with his wife, Sonia, and their children, and Sanjay's cremation had to be put off for a day to allow for their return.

In the early afternoon, Mrs. Gandhi went back to the site of the crash. She walked up to a rope cordoning it off, jumped over the rope, and went up to the officials investigating the crash. "Sanjay was wearing a wristwatch and had a bunch of keys," she said. The officials informed her that they had found the watch and the keys and had deposited them at the local police station. Without further ado, Mrs. Gandhi returned to the hospital.

The capital was soon abuzz with rumors:

"She returned for the watch because on its back are engraved the numbers of Sanjay's secret Swiss bank accounts."

"The keys are to Sanjay's secret cupboards holding tens of millions of rupees."

"The watch and keys were two things that Sanjay wouldn't even allow his wife to touch."

The explanation for Mrs. Gandhi's return to the site so soon after the crash may have been nothing more than that a grief-stricken, benumbed mother wanted some mementos of her son, but many people, including a number of the family's most loyal supporters and retainers, thought that she wanted the watch and the keys because they provided access to some illegal hoard of Sanjay's.

In the afternoon, Sanjay's body was moved from the hospital to the annex to the Prime Minister's residence, where, in all but name, it lay in state—an honor ordinarily reserved for the Prime Minister or the President.

In life, Sanjay had been portrayed for the most part as a gangster figure who raked in money under the table for his mother's political campaigns, rode roughshod over the law, and gave himself airs as his mother's dauphin. But in death he was paid homage worthy of a national hero. Newspapers brought out special editions with black borders and banner headlines ("SANJAY GANDHI DIES IN PLANE CRASH. TRAGIC END OF METEORIC CAREER"). Stock and commodity exchanges were closed; in a number of states government offices were also closed and flags lowered to half-mast; one state shut down schools and universities for several days; another state proclaimed an official three-day mourning period. Throughout the country, organizations of many kinds issued statements and passed resolutions, often professing that they saw in Sanjay's death the loss of their champion. (The president of the Federation of Associations of Small Industries of India said, "He was . . . a young entrepreneur bubbling with enthusiasm to serve the country. In him the small sector has lost one of its well-wishers, friend, philosopher, and guide.") Glowing tributes arrived from leaders of neighboring countries. (The Prime Minister of Sri Lanka said, "Sanjay Gandhi symbolized the hope and aspirations of his generation and his passing away is a loss not only to India but to the youth of the world.") Within hours of the crash, Parliament convened and paid tribute to Sanjay: the chairman of the upper house said, "He was like a shining light in the darkness and despondency. . . . We are poorer, much poorer, after his departure;" a leading member of the opposition in the lower house said, "He rose like a meteor and disappeared likewise." Parliament adjourned for a day in his honor. The Cabinet met and passed a resolution of condolence; the Minister of Agriculture termed Sanjay's death "the biggest tragedy of this century for the people of India."

The day after Sanjay's death, former President V. V. Giri died. Besides having been the titular head of the country between 1969 and 1974, he had been an important figure in Mrs. Gandhi's rise to preëminence in Indian politics. But even the news of

Giri's death was eclipsed by the national mourning for Sanjay.

Meanwhile, Rajiv and his family had arrived in Delhi in the middle of the night (an Air-India flight from New York had been diverted to Rome to pick them up), and Rajiv had gone early in the morning to inspect the spot where Sanjay was to be cremated. Mrs. Gandhi had decided to cremate Sanjay at Shantivana (Peace Ground), on the west bank of the sacred Jumna River, where Nehru had been cremated; and since the evening of Sanjay's death hundreds of laborers from several government departments and agencies had been busy constructing the cremation platform—along with an enclosure for V.I.P.s, diplomats, guests, and the press—beside the venerated site of Nehru's cremation. But Mrs. Gandhi's decision had stirred up something of a political storm, even in the generally reverent atmosphere. Some Janata and Lok Dal politicians were heard to mutter that Sanjay had held only one public office—his seat in Parliament—and that for less than six months, while Nehru had been a founding father of independent India as well as its Prime Minister for seventeen years; cremating Sanjay at Shantivana, they claimed, would be like treating a national shrine as a family cremation ground in the service of dynastic ambition. Rajiv had the laborers dismantle the platform and the enclosure, and reërect them sixty metres behind Nehru's cremation site.

In the evening, Sanjay was cremated on the new platform, which stood five feet high and was fifteen feet square. As Rajiv lit the pyre, Army helicopters flew in formation overhead, the three chiefs of the armed services, standing in the V.I.P. enclosure in full dress uniform, saluted, and crowds shouted, "Sanjay Gandhi is immortal!" (Saxena was cremated privately that day.)

In the following days, all the major English-language national dailies, which had denounced Sanjay during most of his life, carried eulogies reminiscent of those following the deaths of Mahatma Gandhi and of Nehru. "Cruel fate has . . . removed from Indian politics the most forceful personality it has known since independence," an editorial in the *Times of India* said. "Indeed, we have not had another political figure like him since Gandhiji burst on the scene with the force of a volcano over six decades ago. . . . [Sanjay] stood like a rock as one storm after another threatened to overwhelm him and Mrs. Gandhi after she lost office in March 1977." The editorial in the *Indian Express* said, "He produced an impressive impact on slum clearance in Delhi and on the birth control movement in India. . . . He was the prophet of change in a country which, more than any other, was resistant to change." The *Hindustan Times* had an editorial saying, "He was forward-looking, dynamic, astute, a man of few words but plenty of action," and its new editor, Khushwant Singh, wrote a personal tribute to Sanjay and put it on the front page of his paper:

> No greater tragedy could have hit India than the passing of this young man on whom millions of Indians pinned their hopes for a better future. As the lights go out of our homes, our hearts go out to Indira Gandhi and Maneka, two-month-old Feroze Varuna [Sanjay's son], Rajiv and Sonia, and Amteshwar Anand [Maneka's mother]. We dip our flags in salute to this intrepid young man. . . .
>
> We bid farewell to our young departed leader with tears that will take an age to wipe off our eyes. His dying has made us rarer gifts than gold. He has laid the world away and poured out the red wine of youth, and given up the years that were to be his.
>
> The best tribute the nation can pay him is to create the India of his dreams: green with teeming forests, cleansed of all the filth in its cities; with small healthy families and smiling happy girls freed of worry over their dowries.

On June 27th, a special train commissioned by the government left New Delhi to take an urn containing some of Sanjay's ashes three hundred and fifty miles southeast to Allahabad—

the ancient place of pilgrimage at the confluence of the Ganges and the Jumna, the two most sacred of India's sacred rivers—for the customary immersion. The urn had been placed under a life-size portrait of Sanjay in a compartment in the train; a photograph of Sanjay had been affixed to the engine; and the train carried some of Sanjay's relatives and friends. (Mrs. Gandhi herself had chosen not to go.) In Allahabad, the relatives and friends, together with local government dignitaries, ceremonially consigned the ashes to the sacred waters. Meanwhile, other special trains were commissioned to carry other urns of Sanjay's ashes to other parts of the country, where other dignitaries ceremonially consigned those ashes to other sacred waters.

Soon government officials, political leaders, and private individuals throughout the country were vying with one another to perpetuate the memory of Sanjay. Every day, it seemed, there was a new full-page panegyric to him, a new road named for him, a new gift made in his name, new land cleared for a memorial. Sanjay events proliferated: there was a Sanjay rally; an industrialist ceremonially renamed a factory for Sanjay; a government official put into motion plans for a Sanjay game sanctuary. The Congress Indira let it be known that it would build thirty-three Sanjay adult-education centers, one for each year of Sanjay's life, and a Cabinet Minister went as far as to propose setting up a Sanjay corner in the lower house. Even many of Sanjay's foes joined in the memorializing movement. One of them—Chenna Reddy, chief minister of Andhra Pradesh—wrote to the chief ministers of all the other states exhorting them to have government projects and schemes dedicated to Sanjay's memory; and, indeed, the state government of Madhya Pradesh began planning for a Sanjay youth-training center, the state government of Orissa for a Sanjay sports complex, the state government of Uttar Pradesh for a Sanjay memorial hospital and a Sanjay fertilizer complex, and the state government of Punjab for a Sanjay village and a Sanjay university with twenty-five branches throughout the country. In other states, a chief minister laid a foundation stone for a Sanjay bridge; a forestry minister opened a Sanjay forest; officials renamed the Bhabha Hydro Electric Station (Homi Bhabha was a well-known Indian scientist) the Sanjay Hydro Electric Station; a state government endowed Sanjay scholarships for aeronautical engineering; one state announced that it was starting a Sanjay car academy. In New Delhi, the municipality began planning for Sanjay clinics and Sanjay neighborhood schools, and made land available to developers at low cost in order to establish a Sanjay Immortal Colony; the Ministry of Information and Broadcasting mounted a "Son of India" exhibition, consisting of fifteen hundred family photographs; Congress Indira set up a series of Sanjay memorial lectures; a sculptor began taking orders for Sanjay statues; and a dancer announced that she would dedicate a dance composition to the memory of Sanjay. In Simla, a producer announced that he was planning a film on Sanjay's life, and in Bombay a film star ceremonially invoked Sanjay's memory at the première of a film. Mrs. Gandhi herself headed a Sanjay Gandhi Memorial Trust, with several Cabinet Ministers as trustees, to coördinate all the commemorative activities in the country. (On the first anniversary of Sanjay's death, her government issued a special Sanjay stamp—an honor traditionally reserved for leaders who had been dead for fifty or a hundred years.) "No emperor, king, or prime minister of this country has been so eulogised and immortalised as Sanjay is being after his death," *India Today* noted sardonically in an article headed "The Sanjay Industry." That may have been an exaggeration, for Mahatma Gandhi and Nehru had been widely and variously memorialized, but it was clear that Sanjay, who in life had been perhaps the most vilified person in modern India, seemed in death to be on his way to becoming a minor Hindu deity.

One of the more personal tributes to Sanjay was a book entitled "Sanjay Gandhi," by his twenty-four-year-old widow,

Maneka. It was issued with fanfare in December, 1980, to com-
memorate what would have been Sanjay's thirty-fourth birthday.
Maneka's book consists mostly of family pictures and bits of
text, like the following poem, written in English (one of many
that Maneka says she used to write and leave on Sanjay's table):

> Sanjay Gandhi, ferocious being
> Who never looks without seeing.
> Whose facts are almost always right.
> Whose judgments almost always bite.
> Who's so totally work-oriented,
> That he's driven his wife demented
> With his fact and figures and complete knowledge
> And his refusal to indulge in "lollage."
> Sanjay Gandhi computer man
> Why can't you be more human?

She gives occasional thumbnail character sketches of her husband, like this: "People mistook his blunt honesty for gruffness,
rudeness, brusqueness, deviousness or whatever else they wanted
to see in him. When he answered questions in a straightforward
manner, they attributed it to his being uncouth and lacking in
sophistication. . . . As a matter of fact, Sanjay understood people
and situations only too well." She offers domestic vignettes, like
this: "I recall the way I got round him to get another dog.
Since I had one already, he was against getting a second. I
changed my tactics and told him: 'At the moment two people
love you—I and Sheba (my Irish wolfhound). If we get another
dog, there will be one more person to love you.' He gave in
readily with a broad smile." (The absence of Mrs. Gandhi from
this company of "people" who loved him was widely remarked
upon in the capital, and was seen as a confirmation of the popular
view that mother and daughter-in-law were staking competing
claims to Sanjay's legacy.) At one point, Maneka observes, "Rud-
yard Kipling could almost have been talking about Sanjay when

he wrote the poem 'If,' " and she goes on to quote the entire poem. (One particular fragment of it seemed to come up whenever one heard Sanjay's name mentioned in a circle of his admirers: "If you can make one heap of all your winnings/And risk it on one turn of pitch-and-toss . . .")

Even in the context of a general outpouring of grief at a mother's loss of a son, and of the ancient Hindu tradition of idolatry and veneration, and even in view of the fact that death initially casts a softer light upon anyone's life, there was something odd in the headlong movement to memorialize Sanjay. And soon some of the newspapers seemed to have second thoughts, for they started printing letters critical of their eulogies. (One correspondent wrote to the *Statesman,* "I fail to understand why his death is 'a great loss to the country' and when he became 'a great patriot and politician.' ") Opposition politicians began decrying the movement as political and politically inspired. They accused editors, officials, and business leaders of trying to curry favor with Mrs. Gandhi and her government by a sycophantic extravaganza of memorialization, and they accused Congress Indira of using a personal calamity to perpetuate itself in power. Within days of the crash, the national council of the Communist Party of India complained of an "orgy of adulation," and the National Executive of the Lok Dal passed this resolution:

> [The Lok Dal] cannot but lodge a vigorous protest at the systematic attempt made by the Central and State Governments to foster a Sanjay legend by throwing all norms and propriety to the winds. . . . It is absolutely impermissible to declare State mourning as was done by several State Governments, to fly the National Flag at half mast, passing of condolence resolution by the Central Cabinet, close Government offices in several places, to run special trains and invite people to travel without ticket, to treat the site of a national monument erected to the memory of a great freedom fighter as a family cremation ground in blatant violation of the re-

publican spirit and democratic standards. . . . In the general atmosphere of adulation and sycophancy that is being deliberately created by the media, the Lok Dal would like to sound a grave warning that outstanding as the services of Pandit Motilal and Pandit Jawaharlal Nehru [Motilal was Jawaharlal's father] were to the national cause and deep as the public sympathy is for Mrs. Gandhi, the country cannot and will not tolerate the equating of the Indira Gandhi family to a royal family.

We strongly resent the presence of the three Service Chiefs in uniform (and not in mufti) their giving a salute at the funeral and the flying of army helicopters.

The National Executive is astonished that all distinctions of nation, State, party and family are being abolished and the republican form is being transformed into a virtual monarchy. Mr. Sanjay Gandhi may have been the Prime Minister's son, but he was not a dignitary of the State, but only a private citizen and we are constrained to say that the use of the machinery of the State for the funeral has been in very bad taste.

Opposition politicians were soon exploiting the fuss over Sanjay's death for their own ends—claiming that if Congress Indira had not been in power his death would have gone unnoticed and uncelebrated, and letting it be known that if they came to power they might rename all the memorials.

Immediately after Sanjay's death, people started pressing Rajiv, Maneka, and Maneka's mother, Amteshwar Anand, to take Sanjay's place. One newspaper noted:

Within a day of the crash, the war of succession was on. The "draft Maneka" campaign had a feverish urgency about it, for there was the possibility of the other faction in the Palace trying to project the other brother, Rajiv Gandhi. For years the two brothers and their wives . . . would sit at the same breakfast table without exchanging even a word. Rajiv and his Italian wife, Sonia, had even gone on record to express their disapproval of Sanjay's "style" and activities. . . .

The interests of Mrs. Anand and the Sanjay cronies coincided. They had to keep Rajiv out. Even before the ashes of Sanjay were gathered, the Maneka caucus had had several rounds of secret meetings at Mrs. Anand's . . . residence to thrash out their strategy.

The public assumed as a matter of course, however, that Sanjay's mantle would be inherited not by his young widow but by Rajiv, even though Rajiv had always been conspicuously uninterested in politics and practically nothing was known about him. In fact, most of what was known about him was gleaned from biographies of his mother.

It seems that just before Rajiv's birth, on August 20, 1944, Mrs. Gandhi had a pang of hunger. "I asked for a piece of toast," she has said. "As I was eating, Rajiv came out. I was so sorry I couldn't finish my toast." Like Sanjay, Rajiv was brought up mostly in the Prime Minister's residence, had an expensive, privileged education, was an indifferent student, and, following his schooling in India, went to England. He entered Cambridge to study engineering but is said to have had a short-lived academic career. It was at Cambridge, however, that he met his future wife—Sonia Maino, a middle-class Italian girl. Mrs. Gandhi at first objected to Rajiv's marrying a foreigner, but she eventually gave her consent, and the couple were married in 1968. Rajiv and Sonia moved into the Prime Minister's residence and, it appears, settled down to a contented family life: they had a son, Rahul, in 1970, and a daughter, Prianka, in 1972. Also in 1972, Rajiv obtained a commercial pilot's license and joined Indian Airlines, the government-owned domestic carrier, as a commercial pilot, at first flying propeller-driven planes— the Dutch-made Fokker and the Indian-made Avro—and then, after jet training, graduating to the Boeing 737.

Almost from the moment of Sanjay's cremation, Rajiv, a shy and retiring young man, was increasingly drawn into politics in spite of himself. While he helped Mrs. Gandhi rule from behind the scenes, he resisted formally entering politics by announcing his candidacy for Sanjay's Parliamentary seat of Amethi—as he was urged to do. He disregarded a petition submitted in August, 1980, by three hundred members of Parliament—all members of Congress Indira—calling on him to take up Sanjay's work, and continued to hold his job as a commercial pilot. He even refused to join Congress Indira. The longer he hesitated to enter politics formally, the more criticism he aroused in the press. "Power without responsibility is a standing temptation to abuse of authority," Sunanda K. Datta-Ray, a respected Indian commentator, wrote in the *Statesman* in April, 1981. "Leaders do not issue orders from behind a mother's skirts. . . . They must operate within the constitutional framework, and be answerable to the people for all they do. . . . Mr. Gandhi should, therefore, either legitimize his position or be seen to surrender all claims to power. . . . Will the real Rajiv Gandhi, therefore, please stand up and declare himself?" Though the constitution requires that a Parliamentary seat be filled within six months, Sanjay's Amethi seat remained vacant for a year almost to the day. (Mrs. Vijaya Lakshmi Pandit, Rajiv's great-aunt and Nehru's sister, wryly observed to me about Rajiv, "When I decided to stand for my brother's seat after his death, I had to fight the by-election within six months.") At last, early in May, 1981, Rajiv resigned from Indian Airlines, joined Congress Indira, and declared himself a candidate for Sanjay's seat. As it turned out, his reluctance, genuine or calculated, worked in his favor. When the by-election was held, on June 15th, he was opposed by thirteen candidates, and he garnered 258,884 votes out of 307,523 valid votes cast. Ten days later, on June 25th, he was made a member of the executive committee of the youth wing of Congress Indira—a position that Sanjay had used to build up national support in the Party and in the country. It was immediately assumed that Rajiv was in place to succeed his mother as Prime Minister, much as Sanjay had once been.

In the meantime, Maneka and "the Maneka caucus" appeared not to have given up hope; they were busy promoting Sanjay's infant son Feroze Varuna as the next Prime Minister. He, too, was growing up in the Prime Minister's residence. In December, 1980, Maneka gave an interview about, among other things, Sanjay, Feroze Varuna, and the Prime Minister's residence to the *Hindustan Times Weekly:*

Q: Was it to set an example of family planning that you waited five years to have a child?

A: Rubbish—I wanted to wait ten years—this baby wasn't planned. I wanted to have my husband to myself.

Q: Does the baby keep you busy all the time now, keep you up at night?

A: He doesn't sleep with me, he sleeps with my mother-in-law. I spend afternoons with the baby.

Q: Did you see Sanjay as a future Prime Minister of India? What qualities did he have that made him a leader?

A: I definitely saw him as Prime Minister of India one day. Oh, not because he had any "divine right" to it, but because he was extremely capable. . . .

Q: Was he a good judge of people?

A: He was, he saw through people, he knew their weaknesses. He had only just begun his work. After some years, a lot more people would have accepted him. There are a lot of peculiar people in politics—not only in India but everywhere—but Sanjay knew how to make the best use of the material we have.

Q: What did you think of Sanjay's daredevilry, in flying, in driving?

A: It wasn't daredevilry so much as reaching the peak of excellence in whatever he did. When he had mastered something, a subject, he went on to do something else. Before it was boats, then dogs. . . .

Q: And cars. . . .

A: Yes, cars—but he'd lost interest in cars after Maruti was taken over, and taken up flying.

On the morning of the crash, the government, suspecting sabotage, ordered a full-scale judicial inquiry and appointed a judge of the Delhi High Court and four aviation experts to conduct it. Within hours, however, the government cancelled the inquiry. The opposition charged in Parliament that the government's action was a form of coverup—that the government knew that the inquiry would have exposed corrupt dealings in the obtaining of the Pitts, and Sanjay's violations of safety regulations in flying it. Although the government insisted that there was "no hanky-panky," one opposition member managed to table some papers in Parliament about the Pitts which indicated that the plane's history was at best murky. It seemed that in October, 1976, a Swiss director of Seymour Shipping, of London, proposed to his fellow-directors that they buy a Pitts from its manufacturer—Pitts Aerobatics, in Wyoming—and present it to Thomas Mouget (India), Ltd., of Calcutta. At least one Indian director of the London company—Swaraj Paul—was a part owner of the Calcutta company, whose overseas directors had supposedly complained that they experienced difficulty travelling in India. Opposition members pointed to the choice of a sports plane and to the fact that Paul was a member of an important Indian business family, which was likely to benefit from putting Sanjay in its debt, and contended that from the outset the Pitts could only have been meant for Sanjay. At the time, Sanjay had just discovered flying as a sport, and even though it was the period of the Emergency, he could not have imported the Pitts himself without raising questions about how he had got the money to buy the plane and how he had managed to circumvent foreign-exchange controls that barred private individuals from importing foreign goods.

For whatever reason, the London company did buy a Pitts S-2A and ship it to India. But the crated Pitts reached Bombay, the port of arrival, early in 1977, around the time Mrs. Gandhi had relaxed the Emergency and called for the March elections. The shipment was impounded by customs, and then Mrs. Gandhi was defeated. During the rule of Desai and of Charan Singh, the crated Pitts lay stored in the port of Bombay while customs officials and the two companies wrangled in the courts of Bombay, Delhi, and Calcutta over its fate. The case took some bizarre turns. At one point, under the threat of confiscation, the London and Calcutta companies apparently changed their story, and said in their court papers that the Pitts had never been intended for India at all—that it had been meant for a company in England, one Kelly Aeroplane, Ltd., and had been shipped to India by mistake. They begged leave of the court, therefore, to reëxport the Pitts to Britain.

In April, 1980, however, two and a half years after the Pitts reached Bombay and three months after Mrs. Gandhi returned to power, the two companies and the government reached an out-of-court settlement, and customs issued the Calcutta company an import license for the Pitts. Its ownership was then somehow transferred to Sanjay, and early in May the crated Pitts arrived at the Delhi Flying Club. There it was quickly unpacked and assembled, by people who had no experience of the Pitts and had only its pilot's handbook and its maintenance manual to go by. Moreover, no effort was made to check the effects on the plane of its long storage in the damp port of Bombay—though, according to Pitts Aerobatics, every component should be checked for corrosion before assembly. Within a week of the plane's arrival at the Delhi Flying Club, the Civil Aviation Department gave it a certificate of airworthiness.

The Pitts S-2A, light, compact, flexible, and sturdy, is a highly sophisticated high-performance competition plane; in fact, it is considered one of the most advanced aerobatic planes ever produced. It is also said to be one of the safest. Pitts Aerobatics boasts that its plant has produced altogether two hundred and twenty-five Pitts S-2As since 1971 and that, as far as is known, no one has ever died or been injured as a result of structural failure or mechanical malfunction. (It was said that Sanjay's Pitts did not catch fire, and that its engine could not have failed, because the plane's propellers were still turning after it crashed.)

Early in May of 1980, J. Zaheer, Director General of Civil Aviation, reportedly wrote to the Secretary of his department warning that Sanjay was not meeting air-safety regulations during his frequent flights around northern India—that, for instance, he was not filing written flight plans, as pilots are required to do. Zaheer said that Sanjay's violation of air-safety regulations put his own life and the lives of others in danger. It was obviously difficult to issue written orders to the Prime Minister's son, so Zaheer wanted the Secretary to ask the Minister of Civil Aviation to take the matter up with Mrs. Gandhi. Because the letter had come from the Director General, the Secretary could not ignore it, and he seems to have reluctantly passed it on to the Minister of Aviation. The Minister of Aviation seems to have reluctantly given it to Mrs. Gandhi. Mrs. Gandhi kept it for a few days and then showed it to Sanjay, who was incensed. Within hours of Sanjay's reading it, Zaheer was sent on forced leave, and G. R. Kathpalia, Sanjay's friend and Zaheer's deputy, took over Zaheer's duties. Thus, it was Kathpalia who was in attendance for Sanjay's final flight.

Between the time Sanjay received his pilot's license and the moment he first took the controls of the Pitts, he had chalked up six hundred and twenty-seven flying hours. His flying experience was practically useless for aerobatics in the Pitts. Even so, Maneka tells us in her book that although he had flown the

Pitts for only six hours, he was already tired of it and had ordered a hang glider. She says he mastered new planes quickly and tired of them quickly. Her statement about his mastering the Pitts may be hyperbole, but something that she says about the meaning of flying for her husband rings true—that for him "there was no freedom greater than the freedom of the open skies." Sanjay lived in a country where hardly anything works, where everything is slow, where pleasures are mostly out of reach. Planes, speed, and pleasure must have been his modern means of escape from the age-old problems of the country. Flying over the heads of the poor people toiling below must have given him a sense of power and authority. Certainly he seems not to have had much patience with his multiplying poor countrymen. In January of 1981, the writer Shiva Naipaul reported in the London *Observer:*

> The sociologist I spoke to at the University of Delhi . . . did not underestimate the political influence of Sanjay Gandhi or try to expurgate him. Personally and politically, he had recoiled from the man. "Yet . . . yet . . . I have to admit it [the sociologist told Naipaul]. Sanjay did express a certain dark side of the Indian personality. Sometimes when you look around you, when you see the decay and the point-lessness, when you see, year after year, this grotesque beg-garly mass endlessly reproducing itself like some . . . like some kind of vegetable gone out of control . . . suddenly there comes an overwhelming hatred. Crush the brutes! Stamp them out! It's a racial self-disgust, a racial contempt some of us develop towards ourselves. That is the darkness I speak about. I detested Sanjay Gandhi but I fear I under-stood him—better, perhaps, than he understood himself."

In the seventies, Sanjay rose to power because he was his mother's son. In the sixties, Mrs. Gandhi was catapulted into the post of Prime Minister with little to recommend her except that she was her father's daughter, and in the late twenties Nehru was catapulted into the leading ranks of Indian politics with little to recommend him except that he was his father's son. Initially, what mattered in all three instances was the exact degree of birth and caste. ("Take but degree away, untune that string, and hark what discord follows.") The *Times of India* wrote in a posthumous editorial abc   Sanjay:

> Sanjay was an extraordinarily handsome man, bubbling over with youthfulness and he came of noble lineage. (He could be regarded as a "pure" Aryan, his Kashmiri mother being Indo-Aryan and his Zoroastrian [Parsi] father being Indo-Iranian in origin.) In India, high birth, good looks and youthfulness are the traditional qualifications for a hero, and Sanjay stood apart from the commonality of people as a prince.

6

Nepotism and Discord

Sanjay's political career and the Emergency that gave rise to it are spoken of as a watershed between an Indian adaptation of British democracy, with an independent civil service, an independent judiciary, and an independent Army, on the one hand, and a homegrown court autocracy, with personal loyalty, personal reward, and personal vengeance, on the other. The two forms had more or less coexisted since Independence, but Sanjay and the Emergency seem to have hastened the disintegration of the institutions inherited from the British. Everything in India has always depended on the government—what school or college one can go to, what job or promotion one gets, whether one is posted in the capital or in some out-of-the-way place with no schools or medical facilities to speak of, what necessary licenses for doing business one can obtain, how much money one has, how well one's children can be married and settled. But since the Emergency the government has been so politicized and corrupted that depending on it these days really means buying politicians and officials, and it seems that nearly every one of them has his price. Examples abound of proud, independent-minded officials who have been broken, and so do examples of venal sycophants and toadies who have got ahead. Politicians, for their part, have taken to setting up slush funds; their rationalization is that they need huge sums of money to wage free elections and to stay in office, and that they are hemmed in by well-meant but unrealistic restrictions on raising campaign funds. Businessmen contribute lavishly to the slush funds; their rationalization is that they are dependent on politicians for ever-proliferating licenses, and that they could not do business at all without good connections. In September, 1981, Arun Shourie, an investigative journalist in India, brought to light one of the more extreme instances of this practice. He disclosed that Abdul Rahman Antulay, a little-known lawyer, who had no political base of his own, and whom Mrs. Gandhi had made the chief minister of Maharashtra after the 1980 state elections, controlled, with his wife, at least five "charitable trusts." Antulay had collected millions of dollars for his trusts from individuals and companies—going as far as to levy a surcharge on every bag of cement allocated by his ministry to building contractors. He apparently gave the impression that his trusts had the sanction of the central government and Congress Indira; indeed, one of his trusts bore Mrs. Gandhi's name. An editorial in the *Statesman* noted, "Many of those who contributed to Mr. Antulay's trusts must have placed their faith not only in the Chief Minister's willingness and ability to offer something in return, but also in the Central leadership to which he owes his office; in the final analysis, they reposed their trust in Mrs. Gandhi."

Corruption has always been a part of the Indian scene. For one thing, poverty loosens scruples; for another, family is the only social security that people have, and nepotism has always been practiced from high to low, from Prime Minister to sweeper. It is sanctified by the caste system and by religion—by karma and dharma (destiny and duty). Indians even make a rational defense of nepotism, and claim that it is legitimate—not corrupt at all. An advertisement for a mere job as government clerk draws applications from thousands of candidates with more or less equal qualifications, they say, so nepotism is as good a method of selection as any. But everyone acknowledges that the scale and degree of corruption since the Emergency are unprecedented. Bribes are openly solicited and openly received. Since the Emergency, even the simplest transaction, like reserving a seat on a train, requires a bribe. The corruption seems to have had the effect of sapping the morale of every section of society, frequently turning officials into supplicants, judges and magistrates into criminals, Members of Parliament and Cabinet Ministers and their families into hooligans.

The deterioration in standards and performance has been given greater momentum, Indians say, by constitutional and legislative provisions that reserve a certain quota of places in schools, colleges, and the government for Untouchables, irrespective of their native endowments or their qualifications. The original purpose of the provisions was to advance by force of law people who for thousands of years had been kept backward by force of religion. But because the number of these Untouchables has grown with the near-tripling of the general population since Independence (they constitute between one-sixth and one-fifth of a population that stands at seven hundred million), the effect, it is said, has been to retard the progress of others. In any event, in various parts of the country Untouchables are rioting to preserve and extend the quota system, and members of higher castes to abolish it, in what amounts to a caste war. In a sense, the war is over nothing, since few Untouchables have the necessary qualifications to avail themselves of the plums reserved for them. Moreover, the government constantly has to try to sort out the more qualified Untouchables from the less qualified, the less backward from the more backward. Because the legally more backward, and thus more deserving, are often actually less deserving, such distinctions seem to have fostered an inner class struggle among the Untouchables as well. In a backward place, the fine distinctions between backward and more backward—however fateful to different groups of Untouchables—seem indeed Orwellian.

Since the Emergency, there has obviously been a precipitous decline in the calibre of people being elected to office. (The chief minister of one state made practically anyone who was anyone in the legislature a minister, with the result that his Cabinet had no fewer than sixty ministers. He dismissed all criticism by saying that just as large planes were an improvement over small planes, so large Cabinets were an improvement over small Cabinets.) The new politicians seem to have little use for the values of public service and public morality—values that had sustained both the Westernized liberal intelligentsia and the visionary nationalists. A change in the calibre of politicians had made itself felt in state legislatures with the first elections in independent India, but for years Parliament, in New Delhi, seemed to be insulated from that change, because there was one ruling majority party, the original Congress, which was more or less automatically returned to power at the center, and its leaders could afford to be discriminating—to give Party nominations to those whom they considered fit for Parliament. In the 1977 elections, the Janata handed out Party nominations indiscriminately—to practically anyone who it thought could noisily exploit the issues of the hated Emergency and Sanjay's Four-Point Programme. With the victory of the Janata, then, there arrived in the capital members of Parliament who, in contrast to their predecessors, were inexperienced and venal. And a good number of the men and women who succeeded these representatives in the 1980 elections were, if anything, more inexperienced and more venal. Sanjay had given them Party nominations because they were his *chamchas*. Scores of these new members of Parliament—"Sanjay spoons"—did not know enough English to follow the proceedings, which are conducted mostly in English, with the result that Parliamentary debates increasingly resembled mob deliberations. With Sanjay's death, his "spoons" lost their

146

raison d'être; they were so different in style and functioning from Mrs. Gandhi and *her* "spoons" that they were referred to in drawing rooms as "the odd spoons." Many of them, like V. C. Shukla, Jag Mohan, and N. K. Singh, were either dismissed or relegated to unimportant positions, without explanation.

Mrs. Gandhi, since her return to office, has used her near-absolute power to reintroduce certain features of the Emergency piecemeal and through the back door. She quickly rammed two Emergency-type laws down the throat of the opposition. One was the National Security Act, which gives her government the power to arrest anyone it likes and detain him for nine months without charge or trial; Mrs. Gandhi and her Ministers said that they needed the act to control "anti-social elements." The other was a sort of Sanjay memorial—an act nationalizing Maruti, Ltd., which members of her government said had an "infrastructure" valuable for government production of passenger vehicles. Both laws opened up old wounds: opposition politicians saw in one the cornerstone of a new authoritarian era and in the other an extenuation of Sanjay's alleged corruption. The laws were attacked in Parliament with such epithets as "black law," "stinking bill," and "fraud, fraud, and fraud." In July, 1981, Mrs. Gandhi's government assumed sweeping powers that enable it to ban strikes in practically all the private and public industries, and summarily to fine, dismiss, or imprison workers who go out on strike in defiance of the ban. Her government claims that it needed to arm itself with such powers in order to maintain essential services in the country, like water and electricity, but the trade unions have condemned the measure as an Emergency-type effort to preëmpt collective bargaining.

Still, everyone says that if Mrs. Gandhi is trying to bring back the Emergency there is little sign so far of its atmosphere of pervasive fear, and everyone says that this is either because Sanjay is no longer on the scene or because Mrs. Gandhi is still reeling from the shock of his death and has lost the will to rule. As long as he was alive, there was an almost palpable presence of fear; rightly or wrongly, he was seen as representing the ruthless side of Mrs. Gandhi, and this was reflected not so much in what he did or did not do—he was on the political scene only very briefly, and did little more than publicize his few, simple ideas—as in what people thought he could and would do. Lately, however, there has been a flicker of new fear, which is connected in general with what the police can and will do and in particular with what some policemen were discovered doing to prisoners in their custody in the Bhagalpur district of the northeastern state of Bihar. It was disclosed in the national press that since October, 1979, policemen in Bhagalpur had been systematically conducting a "campaign of blindings"—had put out the eyes of at least thirty-one prisoners in their custody, by means of sulfuric acid, bicycle spokes, syringes, or hooked needles. Moreover, it appeared that the blindings had been carried out with the knowledge and the encouragement of police and state higher-ups, who felt that law and order had been breaking down since the end of the Emergency and could no longer be upheld by lawful means. They hoped by the blindings to spread terror in the community and so reverse the deteriorating law-and-order situation.

At first, not only the police and state higher-ups but also the people of Bhagalpur tried to suppress the facts about the blindings. Indeed, the story might never have broken if it hadn't been for a dissenting high jail official, who took testimony from the blinded prisoners and made it public. Despite weeks of a sustained campaign in the national press, with front-page headlines, interviews, and pictures of the blinded prisoners, the police maintained that only the most hardened criminals were blinded, and that they were blinded not in custody by policemen but in the lanes and bazaars by the aroused populace, in a sort of working out of natural justice. Moreover, the entire Bhagalpur community demonstrated repeatedly for the probity of the police and against the intrusion of the national press, as if any methods, however repugnant, that helped or seemed to help control crime were justified. The state authorities refused to investigate any charges or to discipline any policemen. The central government, too, tried to ignore the issue. (The Minister of Information and Broadcasting, Vasant Sathe, contended that the exposure of the blindings would demoralize the police force.) Eventually, the issue reached Parliament and the Supreme Court, and the state authorities were forced to act. They arrested fourteen Bhagalpur policemen while the charges against them were being investigated, whereupon the All-India Policemen's Federation, the police union, threatened to start a countrywide agitation. As a result of that threat, nearly all the suspended policemen were reinstated after a discreet interval.

Like the majority of the prisoners in Indian jails, the blinded prisoners were apparently not convicts but "under-trials"—people who had been rounded up and detained but had not yet been tried for any crime, much less convicted. With the passage of the National Security Act, anyone is liable to preventive detention, and the Bhagalpur blindings have turned jails into symbols of the terrors of that law. Indian jails, though they are notorious for their brutal treatment of criminals, have traditionally been esteemed for their humane treatment of political prisoners. Since the days of Mahatma Gandhi, politicians have sought out jails, because a jail sentence has signified principle, self-sacrifice, and renunciation of worldly attachments. The blindings, however, have spread alarm among politicians of every stripe, and they are trying to exploit the issue for reasons of personal safety as much as political gain.

In many respects, Bhagalpur is typical of the country at large. It is a backward agrarian district of Bihar, and Bihar is a poor state with a sizable population of tribal peoples who are considered Untouchables. In Bhagalpur, there are a lot of low-caste, landless laborers and high-caste landowners, and caste feuds are as common as dust and flies. The terrain, pockmarked with ravines and marshes, is an ideal hiding ground for brigands and gangsters, and bands of them roam through the countryside with impunity, intimidating and exploiting, terrorizing and killing. In India, there is often a tacit alliance between criminals and politicians: they protect each other—one group relying on political protection for survival, the other on crime to produce money for political campaigns. But it seems that in Bhagalpur that alliance was broken in 1979, when a gang murdered the brother of an important local politician. The end of the alliance was apparently the beginning of the campaign of blindings.

The ostensible reason for Mrs. Gandhi's proclaiming the Emergency was political unrest. In many ways, there has been manifestly greater unrest following the Emergency than there was right before the Emergency. It seems that every day there is a new outbreak of unrest within one small group or another. One day, venders somewhere, working the pavements illegally, protest against policemen who are constantly extorting money from them. The next day, in a tribal settlement somewhere else, wives of tribesmen band together and demonstrate to close the liquor shops, because their husbands are squandering the family livelihood on drink. The day after that, some villagers in a forest start a "sticking to a tree" movement, in which each villager wraps himself around a tree to save the forest from the saws of contractors, after appeals to them and to government officials and politicans have failed. Furthermore, the unrest in the country at large before the Emergency was confined mainly to workers and students in the cities, whereas since the Emergency it has seemed to involve also the agrarian masses in many rural areas. During the winter of 1980–81, in the western state of Maharashtra, farmers were demonstrating and protesting against the government—refusing to pay property taxes, blocking roads, picketing officials, organizing marches. Many of the farmers, well-heeled enough to use modern methods, said that the prices they were paying for fertilizer, diesel fuel, and electricity had gone up much more sharply than the prices they were receiving from the government for their onions, sugar cane, and other produce. (The government buys a certain quota of farm produce, which it then markets through its fair-price, or ration, shops.) The farmers were demanding higher prices. The government conceded that it was holding down prices artificially, but it contended that if it were to give in to the farmers' demands there would be uncontrollable inflation, and the first people to go to the wall would be the really poor, compared with whom the protesting farmers were rich. Like many recent agitations, the farmers' agitation in Maharashtra began as an extrapolitical movement, with specific grievances and specific demands, but was soon joined by opposition politicians, who courted arrest en masse and, when they were arrested, cried "Emergency!"—even though during the Emergency they had spent months in jail and this time they were out in a matter of hours. The farmers and opposition politicians were using Mahatma Gandhi's civil-disobedience tactics to bring economic life to a standstill. But the opposition politicians tried to give the struggle a religious character—Hindu farmers fighting against the state government, which was led by a Muslim chief minister, Abdul Rahman Antulay—so raising the most explosive issue in Indian politics and obscuring the grievances and demands that had started the farmers' agitation. Basically, though, the politicians had seized upon the agitation as a chance to foster popular discontent with Mrs. Gandhi's elected government. (In this, they were only doing what Mrs. Gandhi had done during the thirty-three months when she was out of power.) Mrs. Gandhi, for her part, tried to defuse the farmers' agitation by transporting much poorer farmers—two million of them, according to some estimates—from near and far to New Delhi and staging a counterdemonstration, to illustrate that she had widespread political support among farmers, many of whom wanted to keep a lid on prices for produce that they themselves had to buy.

Observers recall that what ultimately made Mahatma Gandhi's movement unstoppable was his involvement of the agrarian masses. But his revolution was peaceful—he was able by and large to control the masses, in contrast to his latter-day imitators, who are not. There is recurrent agitation by farmers in Tamil Nadu which has been violent almost from the start, with the farmers rioting regularly and the police firing on them regularly. All the various farmers' agitations thus carry with them a threat of ever-widening disturbance, which neither the government nor the opposition politicians may be able to control.

At the same time, there is another kind of agitation heating up. From the time of Partition, the northeastern part of the country has been in turmoil because, over the years, millions of refugees fleeing persecution or poverty in what used to be East Pakistan—and since 1977 has been Bangladesh—have been pouring across the border. Bangladesh and India have a border of sixteen hundred miles, which meanders through rivers, streams, marshes, hills, forests, paddy fields—dividing villages and, in some cases, even houses and wells. Most of it is not patrolled, either because it is unpatrollable or because patrolling it would be too expensive. Many of these refugees are Hindus and were part of the first waves of immigrants, who came in the late forties and the fifties, right after Independence, and so they have legal status because of the Partition settlement. Other refugees were part of later waves of immigrants, also Hindus, who at the time of Partition had chosen to remain in East Pakistan but were driven out in the sixties by Muslim persecution, and they also have some kind of legal status, because of a humanitarian policy that India has followed toward refugees all along. Still other refugees belong to still later waves of immigrants, who arrived after the formation of Bangladesh, but many of them are Muslim Biharis who were driven out by Muslim Bengalis. Others are Hindus who sought better economic prospects in India. Many of these later waves of immigrants inundated the state of West Bengal, and from there they moved into the neighboring state of Assam, which was less densely populated than West Bengal and economically better off. In fact, some of the immigrants were induced to come to Assam from West Bengal—or directly from Bangladesh—by agents of Assamese merchants, contractors, landlords, and politicians, who saw in them a ready pool of cheap labor or an automatic bank of votes. In Assam, the presence of the immigrants has had the effect of crowding available land, denuding forests, and straining resources, and so debasing the economic standards of the Assamese. Seven and a half million of Assam's nineteen million people are thought to be Bengalis. Of these Bengalis, five million, the Assamese claim, are illegal immigrants. No one really seems to know the exact number or the precise classification of all the immigrants, but since December, 1979, the Assamese have been bringing practically the entire state government and economy to a halt by demonstrating and agitating to be rid of all the "foreigners." As it happens, Assam ordinarily supplies India not only with much of its tea and some of its timber but also with half of its domestically produced oil, and so far the disturbances have cost the country almost a billion and a half dollars in lost oil production. The country has been forced to spend valuable foreign exchange to replace the oil from abroad, and since the outbreak of the Iraq-Iran war foreign exchange and foreign oil have both become scarce, for Iraq was one of India's main sources of oil and Iran one of its main trading partners. Over the months, the Assamese protesters have sent up a demand for "Four 'D's"—asking the central government to detect all the immigrants, to disfranchise them, to deport them to Bangladesh, and, where that is impracticable, to disperse them to other states. In response, first the central government declared Assam a "disturbed area," and used troops to maintain law and order.

Then the state government also introduced some Emergency measures, like press censorship, but it did not succeed in stemming the agitation. Finally, in June, 1981, the central government accepted the resignation of the state government and put Assam under the direct Presidential rule of New Delhi, but it actually has no answer to the "Four 'D's" demands. Even if all the immigrants could somehow be detected and some understanding reached about which of them should be disfranchised (the protesters insist that all those who have come in since 1951 are in the country illegally, while the authorities are prepared to concede that perhaps all those who have come in since 1971 may be there illegally), that would be only the beginning of a solution, for Bangladesh does not want any refugees back—it does not even acknowledge the existence of any Bangladesh refugees in Assam—and even if they could somehow be dispersed elsewhere in India, that would only transfer the Assamese problem to other states. And lately there has been a new turn in the Assamese situation: some Assamese extremists have made it known that they do not wish their state ever to share its oil with the rest of the country.

The economic blackmail of the Assamese is working, and the central government is wary of stoking the embers of discontent, for fear they might burst into some kind of a secessionist blaze. For the Assamese unrest, which was once based essentially on an economic grievance, has grown into a jingoistic assertion of Assamese language, culture, and ethnic characteristics. Other states in the northeast are seething with their own jingoistic movements, some of them more violent, and overtly secessionist. Such parochial movements are not unique to the northeast, of course (far to the west, in the Punjab, the Sikhs have stepped up their agitation for a national homeland)—or, for that matter, to India. But the difference is that in Assam and elsewhere in the country people by and large live on the very edge of survival, and the smallest amount more for one group can spell disaster for another.

The incidence of violent outbreaks everywhere seems to be growing. In one place or another, Hindus kill Muslims, Muslims kill Hindus, villages of Untouchables are razed, landlords attack Untouchables, policemen and lawyers fight, farmers cut off supplies of food and milk, workers go out on strike, poor people riot, students close down universities, people attack shopkeepers, tribal gangs ambush officials. However widespread the violence seems from daily reports, there is probably still more violence at large, since many incidents of violence must go unreported. The government responds with curfews, commissions of inquiry, investigative reports, but the general impression is of a country in the throes of great unrest. In surveys of the nineteen-seventies which have been published in Indian newspapers and magazines, words that cropped up frequently were "turbulent" and "troubled," and "lawlessness," "disorder," "anarchy," and "breakdown." Furthermore, every day there are reports of rail accidents, bus accidents, boat accidents, pollution accidents. (In June, 1981, more than eight hundred people were killed when a train ran off a bridge in Bihar, and in the following month more than three hundred people in the southern state of Karnataka died from drinking poison moonshine.) There are also reports of mine disasters, hailstorms, landslides, and floods. (In July of 1981 alone, floods in Uttar Pradesh, Bihar, and Assam made three million people homeless, ruined crops, drowned cattle, destroyed oil installations, and washed away roads.) Of course, every country has such calamities, but in India the scale of the calamities is often overwhelming. Perhaps the greatest calamity is the growth of the population, with the consequent disruption of the natural cycle—the disappearance of trees and forests, the erosion of topsoil, the pollution of rivers—which means more droughts, more floods, less food to eat, less oxygen to breathe.

As the unrest and the crises grow, the old British idea that the millions in India are like dumb animals who will respond only to "the stick" is being revived. In groups as different as the Westernized, liberal intelligentsia and the followers of Mahatma Gandhi, there is suddenly muted heretical talk about the benefits of the Emergency—the stick—which they castigated when it was in force. They recall it now with nostalgia, talking longingly about a government that would work, would do something, would give the country a direction. Some of them even speak with grudging admiration of Sanjay, because he instinctively understood the principle of the stick. Khushwant Singh spoke for many of them when he told Shiva Naipaul, "There's no way of clearing slums in this country except by force. If you went through the normal legal processes you could spend the rest of your life. So what do you do? You just *bulldoze* them. Same with sterilisation. You just take them and forcibly *do* it." The atmosphere is charged with expectation, as it was before the Emergency, and the expectation is that Mrs. Gandhi will bring back the stick. She has revived a theoretical debate about the best form of government for a poor society; the same sort of debate preceded the Emergency, as if she wished to justify it before she launched it, and continued during it, as if she wished to defend it once it was in effect. Mrs. Gandhi claims this time around, as she did then, that the fruits of the Indian constitutional democracy are within the reach only of the well-to-do—that a more authoritarian form of government would better serve the needs of the Indian poor—and she asks whether the constitution should be amended accordingly. She has said, "We are prisoners of our constitution." Opposition politicians charge that such talk is self-serving and only cloaks a wish to be proclaimed dictator for life—that the theoretical debate about the ideal constitution can only obscure the urgency of the problems at hand. The eminent jurist Nani Palkhivala, for instance, said in addressing a convention of lawyers in December, 1980, "When your house is on fire, you do not sit down to decide whether your bedroom should be converted into a study."

Mrs. Gandhi has the votes in Parliament and in the state assemblies to amend the constitution and settle the debate. The main obstacle confronting her is the Supreme Court's interpretation of its Keshavanand Bharati decision some years earlier; it was handed down during the euphoria that followed the overthrow of the Emergency, and it holds that the government cannot amend the constitution in a way that will change its fundamental character, as it tried to do during the Emergency. Still, the Supreme Court proved compliant to Mrs. Gandhi's will during the Emergency and would probably prove so again—for in the first year of her return to office she had the opportunity to fill five of its eighteen seats. So people are convinced that Mrs. Gandhi will one day restore the rule of the stick; they say that if she doesn't she will be overthrown sooner or later by some sort of coup, probably led by the military. But authoritarian and military solutions to political problems have been tried piecemeal in India and wholesale in neighboring countries, with deleterious results: superficial stability and order were achieved mainly by pushing the forces of change and turmoil undergound; the ensuing complacence of the authorities and the postponement of a real political accommodation only succeeded in making the eruption, when it came (as in the breakup of Pakistan, in 1971), more violent.

The truth may be that in a poor country what might be called tribal loyalties so fragment the nation that the only substitute for internal warfare is some kind of democracy—political debate serving as a safety valve for volatile parochial emotions. And India is extremely poor and extremely fragmented; in fact, it has more poor people than perhaps any other country has had in the history of the world, and is fragmented by race, religion, region, language, and a feudal class structure. The only parallel in modern times is the twentieth-century Austro-Hungarian Empire, and that empire broke up into a half-dozen political entities. But the parallel may be misleading, for, unlike the conservative, monarchic Austro-Hungarian Empire, India is a parliamentary democracy; has the stability of ancient Hinduism, the religion of the majority; is a modern industrial country with a gross national product that ranks ninth in the world; and has a nuclear capacity.

India exploded its first "nuclear device" underground, at Pokharan, in the Rajasthan desert, in 1974, but it is not clear what its exact nuclear capacity is. (The government has insisted all along that the explosion was for "peaceful purposes.") It is generally believed that India has the industrial and scientific knowhow to build, stockpile, and deliver nuclear weapons. (By some estimates, the nation ranks next to the United States and the Soviet Union in its number of highly trained nuclear scientists.) Since Mrs. Gandhi returned to power, it has seemed that she has decided to "go nuclear" in a big way, for several reasons. One is that Pakistan is reported to be busy making its own nuclear bomb. Since Pakistan has very little industry of its own, a nuclear explosion there, if it comes, may be scarcely more than a political statement. Still, by some estimates Pakistan, once it has succeeded with its first nuclear explosion, will be capable of making two nuclear bombs a year. Mrs. Gandhi told Parliament in May, 1981, that if Pakistan exploded a bomb India would "respond in an appropriate way." A second reason is that the Reagan Administration, which regards Pakistan as a major citadel standing against the expansion of the Soviet Union, has decided to give it military and economic aid amounting to three billion dollars between 1982 and 1986, including the sophisticated, lethal F-16 fighter-bomber—the plane used by Israel to knock out the Osirak nuclear reactor in Iraq. Indians fear that American military aid to Pakistan will be turned against India and may lead to attacks on Indian nuclear sites. In fact, since the *rapproche-ment* between the United States and China in 1971, India has feared an axis of Pakistan and China—India's other enemy, which already has a nuclear capacity—and the Reagan Administration has exacerbated those fears by agreeing to lift the ban on the sale of arms to China. In the early months of 1981, both Pakistan and China moved, in different ways, to thaw their relations with India. But these moves, though they were welcomed in New Delhi, aroused suspicion that their aim might be to lull India into military complacence. The Reagan Administration's policies toward Pakistan and China have therefore had the effect of draw-ing India closer to the Soviet Union, which apparently stands ready to help India go nuclear. A third reason stems from the suspension, early in 1981, of shipments of enriched uranium that the United States had been providing to India, under a 1963 coöperation treaty between the two nations, for fuel for India's only functioning nuclear power plant using enriched ura-nium—at Tarapur, near Bombay. The shipments had come under increasing Presidential and congressional criticism, because India consistently refused to sign the Nuclear Nonproliferation Treaty and, more important, because India also refused to permit inter-national inspection of its nuclear sites to see whether the spent American fuel from Tarapur was being reprocessed to make nuclear explosives. Mrs. Gandhi's government has been lobbying behind the scenes to get the United States to resume the ship-ments, while the Indian opposition has set up a clamor against any form of nuclear dependence on the United States. In April, 1981, the respected opposition leader Subramaniam Swamy said, "The way to handle the U.S. is to act like a big country, not like a petitioning country. The question we must ask ourselves is, 'Are we always going to be a petitioning power, or are we going to play a power role?'" He argued that India should become an independent nuclear power. A month later, another respected opposition leader, Krishan Kant, went further, if anything, saying that India must "prepare for a hydrogen explosion in the shortest possible time." It seems that there is hardly any support in either the Reagan Administration or the United States Congress for the resumption of the fuel shipments, that Mrs Gandhi knows it, and that the Indian opposition leaders, who can speak without the diplomatic constraints imposed on her, are only voicing her own views.

If Mrs. Gandhi does go nuclear in a big way, it appears that—whatever her specific reasons—she will now have both an international justification and a national consensus for doing so. Anyway, the ground has been prepared for the introduction of a nuclear-arms race into the turbulent politics and religious conflicts of the subcontinent.

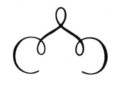

Index